CATCHING UP

REMEDIAL EDUCATION

John E. Roueche

R. Wade Kirk

CATCHING UP:

REMEDIAL

EDUCATION

Jossey-Bass Publishers
San Francisco • Washington • London • 1973

The Jossey-Bass
Series in Higher Education

JOHN E. ROUECHE, *University of Texas*

Consulting Editor, Community and Junior Colleges

For L. D. Haskew

PREFACE

An awakened social conscience during the decade of the sixties brought a national commitment to extending post-secondary educational opportunities to everyone. This commitment was reinforced by a special report of the Carnegie Commission on Higher Education (1970), which recommended that a public community college be established within commuting distance of every potential student by 1980. This goal has already been achieved in several states.

During the sixties the community junior colleges enjoyed their greatest growth—both in numbers of students enrolled and in new institutions established. Because of the widely proclaimed open-door admissions policy, many of those who entered community colleges were low-achieving, nontraditional students (Moore, 1970, refers to them as *high-risk students.*) who had little chance of achieving academic success in traditional colleges. In an effort to accommodate these "new" nontraditional students, community colleges initiated special courses and programs. At first they were called remedial courses. More acceptable, and more common, terms today include developmental, basic, or general studies programs.

Yet, during the same decade, several national, regional, and state surveys revealed the unwillingness of community colleges to provide effective programs for the high-risk student. Despite the paucity of evaluative research on established programs, the evidence was strong that such programs had done little to eradicate the problems of nontraditional students. The general ineffectiveness of compensatory education and remedial programs has been well documented (Roueche, 1968; Moore, 1970). Indeed some evidence suggests that most remedial programs developed during the 1960s consisted mainly of watered-down versions of regular college-level courses (Roueche, 1968). Those courses were primarily preparatory in nature and were organized and taught by the regular academic departments in the college. These early programs were poorly planned and even more poorly implemented.

Some community colleges have now changed this embarrassingly dismal educational picture. New comprehensive programs include a broad range of educational services and learning strategies, and separately organized divisions of remedial education have all-volunteer teaching and counseling staffs. As these new remediation efforts are made, new evidence is required to assess their effectiveness.

As a result of a study on remedial education (*Salvage, Redirection or Custody?*) completed in 1968, the senior author was invited to scores of community colleges across the nation to take a look-see at some new programs for nontraditional students and to evaluate others. In these visits he was impressed with the designs and learning strategies being incorporated and decided in 1972 to do a second study of the effectiveness of selected innovative community college programs for nontraditional students. He determined to identify "successful" programs and then report on the measures of success of each program. He also sought a variety of rationales and organization structures since so many "innovative" programs were developing almost daily.

In the spring of 1972 he wrote to several colleagues asking them to assist in identifying community colleges with well-conceived programs for nontraditional students. More than forty innovative programs were nominated by this process. Seeking to look at programs in existence for three years or more, he narrowed that number to five and still managed to include a variety of program designs and structures, and rural as well as urban colleges.

The community colleges involved were Tarrant County Junior College (South Campus), Fort Worth, Texas; El Centro College, Dallas, Texas; San Antonio College, San Antonio, Texas; Southeastern Community College, Whiteville, North Carolina; and Burlington County Community College, Pemberton, New Jersey. These colleges were selected for several reasons. First, each college enrolls significant numbers of nontraditional students. Second, each has developed a distinct yet innovative approach to remedial education which permits comparisons among different programs. Third, because each remedial program had operated for three years, we could follow students through each college during that time period. Most of the other colleges nominated were in the first or second year of program implementation. Though in close geographic proximity, Tarrant County Junior College, El Centro College, and San Antonio College have entirely different approaches to the nontraditional student. Finally, and perhaps most important, all five colleges are making significant curriculum and instructional innovations in other areas.

The junior author assessed programs in the Texas Community colleges selected. A research proposal we submitted to the Bureau of Research, United States Office of Education

Preface

(USOE), was funded, allowing us to investigate the colleges we selected outside Texas.

It would be difficult to cite all those who assisted us, but we do want to acknowledge the cooperation of the following persons, without whose help the study would have been impossible: President Charles McKinney, Charles Johnson, director of basic studies, Marilyn Monger, acting director for 1971–1972, and Dean Dan McLellan, all of the South Campus, Tarrant County Junior College; President Donald Rippey, Associate Dean Ruby Herd, Dean Bud Palmer, and the guided studies staff at El Centro College; President Wayland Moody, Dean Paul Culwell, and Program Director Catherine Moore of San Antonio College; President Thomas Cottingham, Dean Walter McGraw, Dean Fred Batters, and Program Director Milton "Bunk" Spann and his colleagues at Southeastern Community College; and President Dean Evans, former dean Jim Hammonds, and associates at Burlington County Community College. Special thanks to all the faculty, counselors, and students who cooperated in the project for their generous investment of personal interest and time.

Special recognition is extended to Thomas Spencer, assistant director for community junior colleges, State Department of Higher Education, Little Rock, Arkansas, and his colleagues Clifton Van Dyke and Leonard de la Garza, who served on the Compensatory Education Project for the Texas Coordinating Board. Their excellent set of recommendations, *Reaching for the Ideal,* served us well in formulating our final chapter, and we are indebted to them for allowing us to incorporate some of their suggestions into our work.

We want to acknowledge the support of the Bureau of Research, USOE, in funding parts of this study. The final report submitted to USOE (Roueche and Kirk, 1972) is now available through the ERIC system.

Preface

To Judy Frieling, who prepared the final manuscript, goes our sincere thanks.

Without the contributions of these colleagues and friends, this volume could not have been written. Since final content selection and emphasis were our responsibility, any shortcomings belong to us.

Austin　　　　　　　　　　　　　　　JOHN E. ROUECHE
March 1973　　　　　　　　　　　　R. WADE KIRK

CONTENTS

CATCHING UP

REMEDIAL EDUCATION

1

THE CONTINUING CONTROVERSY

The community junior college through its open-door policy promises educational opportunity for all people. While this philosophy is essentially what has made the institution alluring and, to some, unique, it is concurrently the point under attack by critics both from within and outside the two-year college fold. Many of them charge that the community college is, in effect, diluting its potential by promising to be all things to all people.

Some of the critics are deliberately antagonistic toward the community college. In his review of Moore's *Against the Odds* (1970), Banks (1971, p. 503) urges taxpayers to read the book so that "they might understand the sorry state of affairs in community colleges." Lynes (1966, pp. 59–60) writes of the unpredictable future of the two-year college: "Its functions are so diverse, its pupils so scattered, and its efforts

1

to be all things to all students so determined that it escapes identification. . . . In general it has been looked down upon by holders of B.A. degrees as a refuge for the stupid, and it has been avoided as a place to teach by most serious scholars."

Devall says simply that in attempting to perform entirely too many functions, the community college has become the "bugaboo in American education" (1968, p. 170). Jencks (1968, pp. 304–305) also expresses a pessimistic view of the likelihood of achieving equality of educational opportunity: "consider the case of the junior college[s]. . . . They offer a variety of curricula, including some designed for the academically apathetic or inept students. Yet the existence of these colleges has not improved the competitive position of the poor in any dramatic way."

Proponents of the community college and its commitment to providing educational opportunity to all also state their convictions in strong terms. These writers insist that the community college not only is but has been the predominant force in democratizing American higher education. Spokesmen for the two-year college movement staunchly proclaim it to be "democracy's college" and the "people's college." In his discussion of community college proponents, Jennings (1970: 17) charges that "they deliberately encourage folk knowledge that there is something for everybody" in the two-year college. A more friendly critic says that community college spokesmen can be characterized by a "lack of genuine self-appraisal" and most often by a "mixture of defensiveness and self-congratulation" (Cohen, 1969, p. viii).

In acerbic tones Jennings (1970, p. 24) derides, then berates, and finally challenges the community college to make good its promises by accepting as "its only viable mission the matching of its pretensions with performance." He states that in attempting to meet the instructional needs of all the people the junior college fails. "It strives for continuities and creates

2

fragmentation. It delivers less than what it so generously promises. It often fails the students who need most help. To those who seek direction, order, goals and purpose, it offers the jigsaw puzzle of an all-purpose curriculum. Its all-purpose curriculum is useless" (p. 18). Jennings (p. 22) maintains that the junior colleges have had "a relatively short, generally affluent life up to now, insulated from criticism mainly by the public relations barrage they maintain." He further states that "if the 'people's colleges' are ever to fulfill their role as pre-eminent *teaching institutions,* then they will need to do far more than rely on the academic mystique, inherited from above, that says all one need do is profess what one is" (p. 23).

Helpful critics Moore (1970), Cohen (1969, 1971), Roueche (1968, 1972), and Knoell (1970, 1971) continue to needle the consciences of community college educators by reminding them that the open-door concept is not yet a reality. Gleazer (1970) writes that the greatest challenge facing the two-year college in the 1970s is that of making good on its promise to provide a meaningful education for all.

Controversy indeed! The open admissions policy has brought about an almost unbelievable increase in community college enrollments. Through purposeful design 80 percent of college-age young people in California enter higher education through the doors of the community junior college; in Illinois, 54 percent; in New York, 50 percent; and in Florida, 69 percent (Medsker and Tillery, 1971, p. 16). The Coordinating Board for Higher Education in Texas (1971) reports that almost half the students entering public higher education in Texas in 1970 enrolled in two-year colleges. Stevenson (1970, p. iv) reports that enrollment in Florida's community colleges increased from 4,000 students in five colleges in 1955 to 120,000 students in twenty-seven community colleges in 1969. Florida's Department of Education (*Education Daily,* 1971) estimates that the 1980 enrollment will double that figure.

Catching Up: Remedial Education

Medsker and Tillery (1971, p. 16) report that approximately one-third of all students entering college in the United States are doing so through the "open doors" of the junior college. And, they keep coming—not only traditional college-bound students, who were brought up to believe that "going to college" is a necessary part of growing up, but, in ever-increasing numbers, *new* students, nontraditional students, students whose parents did not attend college, students who in their wildest moments of fantasy never gave serious thought to attending college.

The new student may be characterized as a low-achieving individual who has experienced little if any success in previous educational endeavors. Moore (1970, Chapter I) aptly describes his plight in *Against the Odds:*

> *He is subjected to deliberate professional neglect. . . . No books are written about him and virtually no research. . . . This student is an afterthought. . . . One of the academic squatters. . . . Treated as the villain rather than the victim. . . . Attitude of his instructors is that he cannot learn. . . . He knows he is not wanted. . . . Hundreds of his questions go unasked, thousands go unanswered. . . . Poor teaching for him is legitimate. . . . He is no stranger to failure. . . . The odds are against him. . . . The new [high-risk] students are those whose erratic high school records, economic plight, unimpressive standardized test scores, and race/cultural/class distinctions succeed in placing them at a disadvantage in contention with the vast majority of students.*

Moore insists that the "odds are that the high-risk student [enrolled in remedial courses] will not be any better off academically after his college experience than he was before he had the experience" (Moore, 1970 p. 3). For this student, learning (or the lack of it) has become a painful and frustrating experience. Yet, these are the students who now flock to the beckoning doors of the community junior college with unexplainable expectations of finding some miracle cure for their academic afflictions.

It is the open admissions policy that encourages nontraditional students to enroll. Indeed, many two-year colleges proclaim proudly that they actively recruit such students into various college programs. Most of the controversy and criticism of the open door seems to be directed at its implied promise that the community junior college will provide successful learning experiences for all students. As Moore (1970, p. 5) emphasizes, "the term 'open door' is hypocritical rhetoric if the student, regardless of his level of achievement, . . . [does not] receive the best education possible in the college commensurate with his needs, efforts, and abilities." We also believe the concept is valid only if students are able to succeed in their educational endeavors.

Advocates of the community college believe it can meet the challenge of providing quality education for low-achieving, nontraditional youth by being a "teaching institution." This claim is reinforced by two-year colleges, who proudly reject the idea of instructors becoming intensely involved in the research-and-publish activity so prevalent in four-year institutions. Supporters of the community junior college take great pains to emphasize that teaching staffs in the two-year college devote full time to teaching.

Accompanying this commitment to competence in teaching is the notion that successful learning experiences for high-risk students can best be facilitated by providing an equally competent counseling staff. Thus, by recruiting instructors who want first and foremost to teach and counselors who possess the special skills and desire to work with educationally deprived students, the community college believes it can deliver on the promise of the open door.

And most colleges have developed special courses and programs to accommodate these students when they enroll. In fact, it has been found that the courses with the heaviest enrollments are those that may be categorized as remedial or compensatory in nature. A variety of terms has been contrived to describe these special courses: *developmental, directed, compensatory, guided, basic,* and *advancement studies.* Whatever the nomenclature, most programs are designed to develop students' basic skills to a level from which they can enter regular college curriculum programs. A careful perusal of recent community college catalogs and a check of student enrollments by course and curriculum reveals that remedial English, remedial reading, and remedial mathematics are probably the most offered courses in American two-year institutions.

The assumption inherent in establishing remedial courses is that chances for academic success in college are greatly enhanced for marginal students because of their having available such programs. Yet, as Schenz (1963), Berg and Axtell (1963), Roueche (1968), Gordon and Jablonsky (1967), and Blocker and others (1965) point out, little hard evidence exists to support the contention that these programs do indeed help the student remove or remedy his deficiencies. In their comprehensive study of compensatory programs, Gordon and Wilkerson (1966, p. 156) report: "Despite the almost landslide acceptance of the compensatory education commitment, we find nowhere an effort at evaluating these innovations. . . . Where evaluative studies have been conducted, the results typically show ambiguous outcomes affecting unknown or amorphous educational and social variables."

Seldom do current research studies contain hard data pertaining to the persistence, academic achievement, or attitude development of students in remedial programs. Perhaps this omission is due to reluctance, lack of expertise, or simply an insouciant attitude on the part of junior college administrators toward keeping statistical records. Of those few studies available we have selected three to summarize. Several other studies at the four-year college level tend to corroborate the findings outlined here.

In their recent and comprehensive review, Kendrick and Thomas (1970, p. 171) observe that "research on the extensiveness and effectiveness of compensatory programs and practices has been limited in quantity and scope. Yet, even with the paucity of evaluative studies, it is safe to note that evidence points to the conclusion that existing compensatory programs and practices have made little impact in eradicating the problems of disadvantaged college students, nor have the majority of colleges accepted this area as their role."

Snyder and Blocker (1970) found in a study of developmental students who matriculated over a three-year period at Harrisburg Area Community College, Pennsylvania, that between 33 and 40 percent of the students did not return for a second year's work. Less than one-fourth of the students achieved at least a C average for the cumulative period of attendance and only 27 percent earned the associate degree.

Ludwig and Gold (1969) reveal that only 37 percent of remedial students at Los Angeles City College achieved a grade average of C or above for the first semester. Only 34 percent ever completed two years of study in college.

From a review of the related research and literature three conclusions can be reached: (1) There is a pronounced lack of research on the effectiveness of remediation efforts in community colleges in terms of assessing academic performance, persistence, and attitudes of high-risk students. (2) Even with the dearth of research the evidence indicates that remedial courses and programs in two-year colleges, and in all of higher education for that matter, have largely been ineffective in remedying student deficiencies. (3) There is an increasing number of critics of the open-door college and its implied promise to provide successful learning experiences for all its students. Focus of criticism seems divided between the over-zealous aims of the junior college and the reluctance of the institution to evaluate its efforts.

Since the publication of the first national study of the effectiveness of remedial education programs in community junior colleges (Roueche, 1968) notable changes have occurred in two-year remedial programs. One important change is the disappearance of the term *remedial* from college catalogs and the professional literature as colleges have modernized their images. Other changes have been more profound. In recent years most community junior colleges have abandoned the process of assigning the least experienced faculty members to teach these nontraditional students in special programs. In fact, faculty assignments are now a rarity. Today's instructor in such programs is most likely a "volunteer"—that is, he requested the position. He is teaching these students because he believes they are capable of achieving. Perhaps most important, today's instructor cares about his students—openly and un-abashedly cares! He wants to help students succeed. This change is a most significant one.

Community junior colleges are pioneering in the development of individualized instructional materials and strategies to better accommodate the entering student where he is—not at some arbitrary starting point. In a pilot survey conducted in Texas this year, we found that the mean level of achievement on the Nelson-Denny Reading Test in community college English courses was slightly above the tenth-grade level. In remedial or developmental courses, the range on the same test was from grade 3 to grade 12. Individualized instructional approaches are necessitated by the unparalleled diversity in the contemporary two-year college student body.

With this instructional development have come changes

in the school calendar. Some colleges now permit students to begin and complete courses at any time during the calendar year. Nonpunitive grading is becoming common, recently spreading to the ivied halls of Harvard. Students who enroll with academic deficiencies in many colleges no longer are faced with the "Scarlet F" if they have not completed all course assignments by the end of a given semester. They simply continue until they meet the necessary course requirements and then proceed to the next course. Use of student tutors is expanding and many colleges report the positive effects of this practice. Peer counseling has also proven to be a successful endeavor in acclimating and orienting the new student to the community college environment. These changes are impressive and obviously were made in efforts to improve program effectiveness. But the *key* question was and is: "How effective are the recently developed programs in contemporary community colleges in meeting the educational needs of the nontraditional, high-risk students now enrolling in ever-increasing numbers?"

Though there have been national, regional, and state surveys made in recent years to ascertain the types of programs, the numbers of students enrolled in them, and the nature of the services provided for nontraditional students, evaluations of their effectiveness are still lacking. Our study aims to help fill that gap. Its purposes are four: (1) To assess the effects of selected innovative remedial education programs on students' academic performance and persistence in college; (2) to determine students' attitudes toward selected aspects of the innovative programs; (3) to identify and describe those characteristics which appear to be related to the success or failure of the program in terms of student attitude, persistence, and academic performance; and (4) to investigate relationships existing among the variables of persistence, academic performance, and attitudes of students of major race-ethnic groups enrolled in the selected programs.

More specifically, we sought to answer the following questions:

1. To what extent do students in the selected remedial programs persist in college?

2. How well do students in remedial programs perform or achieve academically in college?

3. Is academic performance of students in remedial programs, as measured by gradepoint average, superior to that of comparable students enrolled in nonremedial programs?

4. Are students in remedial programs more persistent, as measured by enrollment in and completion of subsequent semesters, than comparable students enrolled in nonremedial programs?

5. To what extent are students in remedial programs satisfied with (a) counselors and counseling, and (b) instructors and instruction?

6. Are there significant relationships among the variables of student attitude, persistence, and academic performance when low-ability students are statistically subgrouped according to major race-ethnic groups?

7. Are there significant differences in persistence, academic performance, and attitude among students in remedial programs at different colleges?

8. Can counseling and instructional procedures be identified which tend to produce increased student satisfaction, persistence, and academic performance?

9. What implications may be drawn from this research for the improvement of counseling and instruction as they relate to remedial education programs in urban junior colleges?

Most innovative programs for nontraditional students are recent developments; hence, little evaluative data exist on their effectiveness. But the real problem is not newness but the fact that in many cases programs have been conceived and implemented with little or no thought given to the systematic collection of data for evaluation purposes. The end result is that program directors, deans, presidents, local boards of trustees, state-level governing bodies, and federal funding agencies still do not have concrete information on which to base policy design, introduce improvement and change in the teaching-learning process, and allocate funds to those programs and approaches which have the best potential for producing successful learning experiences for high-risk students.

Remediation efforts, until at least three years ago, consisted largely of watered-down versions of regular college courses. Each department of the college assumed responsibility for organizing and teaching the course, and in many instances instructors believed that the integrity of the department and the scholarly content of the discipline must be protected. Students, meanwhile, continued to fail and to resent even more the subject and the traditional manner in which the educational process was conducted. Instructors were assigned to remedial courses based on the pecking order of seniority and tenure within the department (Roueche, 1968, p. 16). Because of the absence of discussion and exchange of ideas among instructors the programs lacked direction, a common philosophy, and administrative leadership. Counselors, already overloaded with students and inured to assembly-line practices in processing students, were indisposed to provide extra time, understanding, encouragement, and special skills necessary for working with low-achieving students. This study was undertaken in order to determine the extent to which the most recent and optimistic approaches to remedial programs have proved effective in increasing persistence, improving academic performance, and cultivating positive feelings toward learning among low-achieving students.

Five colleges were selected for this study from a list of more than forty innovative colleges nominated by junior college presidents, deans, and various university-based junior college professors who were asked to name colleges that had a reputation for having developed imaginative approaches to programs for nontraditional students. Obviously this selection process omitted many fine programs that have not benefited from the same press coverage as those colleges nominated for our study. But, in defense of our selection strategy, we were looking for the best programs we could find, realizing that few of the colleges had evaluation data available with which to select "the best."

Many colleges were eliminated from the present study because their innovative programs were begun too recently. We sought programs that had been in operation for a minimum of three years. Outside of the colleges included in this study, we found no others that met the requirements of both innovativeness and three-year existence.

The fact that several of the colleges are located in Texas is not to suggest that Texas necessarily has a greater number of successful programs than other states. The Texas schools were included not just for the convenience of the authors but because each had a different set of assumptions behind its program and all employ various organizational devices to "get the job done." Three of the five colleges have an urban setting, while two are located in rural or semirural settings. All have established widespread reputations for implementing effective programs for nontraditional students.

In this report, we seek not only to describe the programs at each college but to report on the success of each.

2

THE PROGRAMS

This chapter describes each of the developmental studies programs at the five community junior colleges selected for study. Included in the descriptions are the following: program objectives; subject areas taught; means of identifying potentially low achievers; qualifications for entering regular college programs; grading policies; counseling and supplementary services provided; instructional methods used; size of programs in terms of student enrollment; race-ethnic makeup of programs and colleges; and mean composite scores of high-risk students on the American College Test (ACT).

These data and related information were obtained from two sources. First, available written materials such as college catalogs, student and faculty handbooks, policy handbooks and statements, program evaluations, and course descriptions were examined carefully. Second, and most importantly, program directors, counselors, and faculty members were interviewed to obtain accurate and up-to-date descriptions of the remedial programs. A cassette recorder was used in the interviews for purposes of reviewing, organizing, and developing narrative descriptions of the programs. Almost all the information presented in this chapter was obtained from in-depth interviews with program personnel at the selected colleges. Only one of the colleges has a body of written materials available on its innovative developmental program.

SOUTH CAMPUS—TARRANT COUNTY JUNIOR COLLEGE

The developmental studies or Basic Studies program, as it is referred to, has a block-type, vertical-team approach operating within a separate division in the college. The program is one year in length, and with the exception of physical education, courses are taught by the Basic Studies staff. According to Tarrant County's description of its program it is "a one-year, college-level program in general education, designed for the marginal or high-risk student. . . . The student is placed in a dynamic environment which provides individualized attention by instructors . . . [and] the use of innovative teaching techniques and an interdisciplinary approach to learning."

Students enroll in developmental studies on a block schedule basis. That is, course selections and course times are predetermined for large groups of students. Five sections of approximately twenty students per section are assigned to a group of six staff members, each of whom teaches a different subject. Students in the same section attend classes as a unit. The group of five instructors and one counselor is called a *vertical team* and is responsible for the educational experiences of approximately one hundred students during their initial year in college. Three such vertical teams exist at the college.

The term *vertical team* is derived from the fact that there are no academic departments within the division of developmental studies. Included on each team are instructors

who would normally reside in the various academic departments of the college if no division of developmental studies
existed. The separate division of Basic Studies is thought to
add strength to the colleges commitment to providing educational experiences to educationally disadvantaged students. At
the time of this study the division of developmental studies
consisted of fifteen instructors, three counselors, and one division chairman. All of these personnel were volunteer staff
members.

College and district administrators and program personnel believe there are several advantages to the vertical-
team approach operating within a separate division of developmental studies. First, flexible scheduling permits allocation
of broader time blocks to activities such as field trips, guest
speakers, group research, independent study, and group
dynamics work. Second, the opportunity exists for strong peer
relationships to develop among students in an intact group.
Third, a team of instructors gets to know students on a personal
basis. Instructors and counselor work together to solve special
learning problems. Fourth, an interdisciplinary approach is
possible when a team of instructors teaches the same students.
The five instructors and one counselor meet often to plan
common units of study and to devise appropriate strategies for
instruction. Finally, the vertical-team approach is viewed as
"an educationally sound and mechanically feasible vehicle"
which permits the program to expand without sacrificing
personal contact with students.

The six major areas of study include communications,
natural science, reading improvement, humanities, social
science, and personality foundations–career planning. The
curriculum is designed around O'Banion's concept (1971) of
a humanizing model of education, wherein the student himself
becomes the center of the curriculum. Topics for study during
the year are based on the individual, his relationship to society,

15

and contemporary societal issues. The two major units of study during the first semester are Who Am I? and Where Did I Come From? During the second semester the units of study include Societal Issues and Problems and Society of the Future.

Courses given in the fall semester are:

Course	Credit Hours	Contact Hours
Communications I	3	3
Reading Improvement	1	2
Social Science I	3	3
Natural Science I	4	4
Humanities I	3	3
Personality Foundations	3	3
Physical Education*	1	3
	18	21

Spring semester courses are:

Course	Credit Hours	Contact Hours
Communications II	3	3
Social Science II	3	3
Natural Science II	4	4
Humanities II	3	3
Career Planning	3	3
Physical Education*	1	3
	17	19

* Students take physical education in regular college classes.

The individual subject areas of the program are integrated through means of a central theme—in this case, the student. In natural science the student studies his physical-biological self in a classroom-laboratory setting. In humanities he studies his personal beliefs as they relate to his values and attitudes. Included are the elements of art, music, literature, philosophy, drama, religion, and film. In communications the emphasis is on improving his writing, speaking, and reasoning skills as they relate to his communications with others. In the reading improvement course efforts are made to analyze and improve his basic reading habits. In social science topics in sociology, anthropology, psychology, economics, history, and government are studied as they affect the socialization process and his relationship to others. In personality foundations–career planning the student examines his own personality development and explores his occupational-career interests.

A student who enters South Campus is advised by the admitting counselor to enroll in developmental studies if his composite score on the American College Test is 13.0 or below or if he scores below the twenty-fifth percentile on the ACT composite predictor score. This predictor score is derived from both the student's high school grades as reported on the ACT Profile Analysis and the composite score on the ACT.

Other criteria established by program personnel as guidelines for admitting students into developmental studies include the following: The student possesses a high school diploma or its equivalent. The student is between seventeen and twenty one years of age. The student had little academic success in high school. The student desires a full-time day schedule. The student aspires toward an Associate in Arts degree or beyond.

The program at South Campus is designed for approximately three hundred high-risk students. Because considerably more high-risk students enter the college than the program can accommodate, the decision was made to restrict further the eligible candidates to younger students and to students who indicated a desire to obtain the Associate of Arts degree. The latter criterion, therefore, excludes those students who indicate upon entry that they wish to pursue technical and vocational programs.

Catching Up: Remedial Education

After completing the developmental studies program the student is recommended to go one of four ways: into a program in which he can transfer to a four-year college or university; into a two-year technical or occupational program leading to the Associate in Applied Science degree; into a vocational program for which he will receive a certificate of completion; or into job training in industry or in the community. Evaluation of the student's progress and abilities is made by the vertical team with whom the student works during the year.

The developmental studies program is designed so that the student earns thirty-five semester hours of college credit, most of which count toward graduation. Should the student choose to transfer, many of these credits are accepted by four-year colleges and universities.

The following objectives are listed for the program: (1) to assist the student in developing group relationships within the college environment; (2) to help the student become more aware of his community, its problems and resources; (3) to assist the student in solving his financial problems while he is attending school; (4) to increase the duration of the student's involvement in college experiences; (5) to help the student cope with his personal and academic problems; (6) to provide a curriculum which is exciting and different from his high school experience in education; (7) to assist the student in realistically assessing his vocational objectives so that they are commensurate with his interests, abilities, and achievement; (8) to improve the student's chances of achieving academic success; (9) to assist the student in developing basic communication skills; (10) and to assist the student in developing a positive and realistic self-concept.

South Campus staff members ask students to evaluate the developmental studies program at the end of each academic year. The ten general objectives delineated above were used by the staff as criteria for determining the effectiveness of the 1970–1971 program. Students were asked to respond anonymously to a questionnaire made up of items reflecting program objectives. South Campus was the only institution studied that systematically evaluated its developmental program each year and officially published the report of this evaluation.

Instructors use Mager's *Preparing Instructional Objectives* (1962) as a guide for defining performance objectives in each of the developmental courses. Instructional packages have been constructed in an effort to individualize instruction for students, and lessons containing factual information have been put on audiotape for use in the Learning Resources Center. Video tape has also been used to teach and point up discussion skills. Field trips and guest speakers have brought the student into close personal contact with the community. In a period of a year fifty guest speakers may be scheduled for the various sections of students. Various group techniques are used when feasible. For example, a small group discussion consisting of a section of twenty students is used when active participation is desired from students. This kind of situation also provides an opportunity for students to assume leadership roles. The lecture group is used for two or three combined sections of students when it is expeditious for an instructor to give information prerequisite for further work. Large group settings are utilized for purposes of hearing a guest speaker at the beginning or completion of a unit of study.

The role of the counselor in the vertical team is considered to be vital. The focus here is on helping the student to view himself realistically and to develop a positive self-concept. The counselor teaches the personality foundations course and the career-planning course taught during the two semesters. He also administers a series of psychological tests, including the Tennessee Self-Concept Scale, General Aptitude Test Battery, Kuder Interest Profile, Beta (non-verbal) Intelligence Test, and the Mooney Problem Check List. Most of these are interpreted for the students in individual or small group counseling sessions. Instructors also receive an interpretation of the results. The Mooney Problem Check List is used only as a counseling device in locating problems in the student's background which may be causing difficulties for the student in school. The counselor works with students in improving study habits and skills. In addition to serving as a confidant for students with personal and social problems, the counselor is also a resource person for students with emotional problems and further acts as a referring agent to appropriate community agencies. Finally, the counselor assists students in planning for a career. Greatest emphasis is given this topic during the second semester. Vocational interest tests are used to help the student plan a program of college studies. Students also research and become familiar with several occupations in which they are interested.

Reflected in Table 1 are data describing the program and sample populations at South Campus. For example, the number of students enrolled in developmental studies decreased during the three-year period considered in this study from 318 to 232. Black students made up 32 percent of the program enrollment in 1969–1970 as compared to a total college black enrollment of 10 percent. Two years later only 17 percent of Basic Studies students were black. Some reports indicated a minority student boycott of the 1971–1972 developmental studies program, which could explain this sharp drop for the 1971–1972 school year.

For purposes of comparing students in developmental studies with those who had similar characteristics but did not enter Basic Studies, a control group of high-risk students was formed (see Chapter Three). Students in this group were 31 percent black, 55 percent white, 7 percent chicano, and 7 percent of other or unknown classification. Black students in

Table 1
Population Characteristics of South Campus Basic Studies Program

Year	Program Size (Fall Term)	Sample Size Original N	Original %	Final N	Final %	Mean ACT Composite Score of Sample	Race-Ethnic Composition (Percent)[a] Black	White	Chicano	Other
1969–1970	318	42	13	36	11	11.2	32	64	4	..
1970–1971	274	31	11	28	10	12.0	28	68	4	..
1971–1972	232	41	18	36	16	10.9	17	78	3	3

[a] Race-ethnic composition of the 1971–1972 program was determined from the sample. Compositions of the 1969–1970 and the 1970–1971 programs were reported by the college.

the 1971–1972 developmental group had an ACT mean composite score of 8.2 (based on sample of six students) while white students had a mean score of 11.1. The ACT mean composite scores for black students and white students in the control group were 10.2 and 11.8, respectively. The mean scores for chicano students and those in "other" classification were meaningless because only a very few students were involved. Total-group scores were 10.9 for Basic Studies (thirty-six students) and 11.2 for control group (twenty-nine students).

The grading system used at South Campus is based on a four-point system and consists of the traditional A through F grades. The only exception to this grading system was the assignment of an "I" grade when the student for valid reasons had not completed requirements for the course.

EL CENTRO COLLEGE

The basic objective of the Guided Studies program is stated simply as making the open-door philosophy of the college a workable one for educationally disadvantaged students. This goal is best accomplished by providing success experiences which help eliminate negative attitudes toward learning. The program attempts to assist students to develop the skills needed to succeed in college and/or on the job.

The El Centro program has existed in its present form, with minor variations, since the fall of 1969. Before that remedial courses were taught in the division of communications and in the combination math-science division. In the fall of 1968 a separate division of developmental studies was organized and the complement of existing courses and services was placed within the division the following year.

Several factors were considered in the creation of a separate division of developmental studies. Administrators and program organizers felt that all personnel involved in teaching and counseling high-risk students should be volunteers. In order to give proper recognition and emphasis to the staff and to the program the decision was made to create a separate division within the college. It was believed that the philosophy and objectives of the program could best be articulated and implemented through this type of organization. More important, there was evidence that the attrition rate for low-ability students was excessively high in those situations where instructors and counselors were rountinely given a remedial course or high-risk students as part of their normal teaching or counseling duties. Some staff members were unwilling to be assigned these duties, while others were unsympathetic toward these students or at least lacked the necessary skills for working effectively with students possessing severe learning difficulties. The negative feelings of instructors were quickly communicated to students. Furthermore, some instructors felt a need to protect the scholarly content of the discipline and this effort often took precedence over attempts to implement effective teaching strategies. In other instances the students were merely subjected to emasculated versions of the regular courses. Whatever the approach, high-risk students prematurely left the college in great numbers.

Another factor in the creation of a single division of developmental studies was the belief that it would be educationally sound for instructors to cooperatively plan learning experiences for low-ability students. Team teaching and interdisciplinary approaches, for example, would enable students to view their classroom experiences and endeavors as having a common purpose rather than as isolated learning tasks.

A final reason for creating a separate division was the belief that misunderstandings which typically exist between counselors and instructors in many educational institutions could be minimized within a single division. Not only would the close proximity of counselor and instructor enhance the possibilities for joint planning and consultation, but even more desirable, a merging of roles might occur.

In addition to these advantages, as perceived by El Centro personnel, the separately organized division of Guided Studies provides other services for students. An open writing laboratory staffed by paraprofessional teacher aides is available for any student needing assistance in the area of composition, and appropriate study materials are provided. Special seminars are conducted by developmental reading staff for students at no charge. Seminars typically range from a few days to several weeks in length and cover such topics as speed reading, comprehension, vocabulary, spelling, study skills, and test-taking skills. Materials used include pre- and post-tests, workbooks, programmed texts, cassettes, and other instructional materials prepared by the staff and various educationally oriented commercial companies. Peer counseling is another service of the division. Students considered to be "people-oriented" are selected and trained by the developmental studies staff. Their training involves, in addition to many hours of familiarization with college catalogs and college programs, an experience in a human relations learning lab and a practicum in which the student counselor serves for a period of time as an aide to staff counselors in small group sessions. Peer counselors work not only with high-risk students but also with other students during periods of registration at the college. In the spring of 1972 some forty-four peer counselors were in various stages of training at El Centro. These peer counselors operate from their own office located in an area of high student activity on the campus.

All students who score 11.0 or below on the composite of the American College Test are required to enroll in developmental studies. College and program officials concede, however, that many students who would normally fall within this category do not enroll in the developmental studies division because of the lack of ACT scores for large numbers of students at the time of entry. Because the institution is a large inner-city community college which actively recruits ghetto/poor students, many enter the college without having taken the ACT. Plans are presently under way at El Centro to administer a test, such as the School and College Ability Test (SCAT), to every entering student who does not possess ACT scores. In this way all high-risk students can be identified immediately.

Characteristics of students in the remedial program at El Centro are shown in Table 2. Program personnel state the primary reason for the reduction in program enrollment over the three-year period was the decreasing number of students who enter the college with required ACT scores. Too, some students who fall below the 11.0 composite score may be placed in regular classes by the admitting counselor if there is some reason to doubt the validity of the score.

As Table 2 shows, at least 54 percent of the 1971–1972 sample of developmental studies students were from minority groups; whereas, according to the Texas Coordinating Board's Compensatory Education Project report (1971), only 20 percent of all students enrolled in Texas junior colleges were minority group members. A report by Crossland (1971) shows the black population in the city of El Centro to be 22 percent of the total population. So we see that blacks and chicanos were enrolled in developmental studies in disproportionately high numbers. The ACT mean composite scores for black students and white students enrolled in the developmental studies program in 1971–1972 were 8.5 and 9.8 respectively. The score for chicanos (based on a sample of five students) was 7.7. The control group ($N = 28$) of high-risk students not enrolled in developmental studies in 1971–1972 was 71 percent black, 14 percent white, 7 percent chicano, and 8 percent unknown. The ACT mean composite score was 8.8 for black

Table 2

Population Characteristics of El Centro Guided Studies Program

Year	Program Size[a]	Sample Size Original N	Sample Size Original %	Sample Size Final N	Sample Size Final %	Mean ACT Composite Score of Sample	Race-Ethnic Composition (Percent)[b] Black	Race-Ethnic Composition (Percent)[b] White	Race-Ethnic Composition (Percent)[b] Chicano	Race-Ethnic Composition (Percent)[b] Other
1969–1970	570	64	11	63	11	9.0	..	..	..	..
1970–1971	467	39	8	36	8	8.0	..	..	..	..
1971–1972	376	45	12	35	9	8.9	40	43	14	3

[a] Includes full-time and part-time remedial program students.
[b] Race-ethnic data were not available for the 1969–1970 and 1970–1971 groups.

students and 10.8 for white students in the control group. As a whole, the remedial group (N = 35) scored 8.9 and the control group 9.5.

Subject areas included in developmental studies at El Centro are reading, writing, mathematics, and a special group guidance and counseling course. A student may be enrolled in one or two courses in developmental studies and also be enrolled in courses in other divisions of the college. He may also enroll for a second semester of reading, writing, and oral communication skills. However, these courses do not count toward college graduation requirements or for transfer purposes to four-year colleges and universities, although they are included when computing the student's gradepoint average.

Two other courses are taught by the developmental studies staff. An advanced reading course, for which graduation credit is granted, is open to any student in the college who possesses basic reading skills and wishes to improve his reading speed, comprehension, and study skills. A second course is offered to those students who wish to obtain a high school equivalency diploma by passing the General Education Development (GED) Test.

The completely volunteer staff of the developmental studies division in the spring of 1972 consisted of nine full-time instructors, three full-time counselors, four paraprofessional teacher aides, and seven part-time night instructors. Student assistants from the college work-study program were also extensively used.

The developmental studies mathematics course was designed for students lacking basic math skills and for those needing review. Students enrolling in this course were generally inept in high school mathematics, were school dropouts, or had been out of touch with the classroom for many years. Diagnostic tests are administered for purposes of identifying deficiencies and planning an individualized program of instruction for each student. Programmed texts are the primary medium for instruction; the student requests tests when he feels ready for them. The basic objective of the course is to enable students to analyze and solve mathematical problems faced in everyday situations, such as figuring interest rates and finance charges, balancing savings and checking accounts, completing tax returns, balancing budgets, and other related consumer problems.

The reading course is designed to improve a student's reading skills in the shortest possible time. The typical student in the program reads at a seventh-grade level. Individualized programs of study are planned for each student after his reading weaknesses are isolated. The student is exposed to a wide variety of reading materials produced by the staff and by several commercial publishing companies. A series of standardized reading tests is used, with accompanying forms and pre- and post-tests. Work for individual students may be concentrated in special areas such as increasing reading speed, comprehension, vocabulary, and word-attack skills. Students are encouraged to read books of their choice. A library of some two hundred paperback books is available from which selections may be made. Monthly book reviews are made by each student and invited faculty members give monthly book reviews to each reading class. Films, workbooks, tapes, records, and prepared cassettes are also used in conjunction with dictaphones, controlled readers, and other mechanical reading aids. Team teaching is used in every class in order that teachers may work with smaller groups and give more individual attention to students.

The writing course takes place in a laboratory setting with the emphasis on each student progressing at his own rate. The student helps to determine the level of competence he wishes to reach. Depending on the academic or vocational plans of the student, realistic goals are then established for him or her. Personal contact between instructor and student is stressed. Teacher aides who possess a minimum of two years of college background in English or reading assist the instructor in each class. Lectures are deemphasized and used only when students need common instruction in major areas of weakness. Programmed tests, staff-prepared materials, and mechanical aids are used to help students increase their writing skills. Individual carrells where students listen to tapes and use dictaphones contribute to the laboratory approach to writing.

The special orientation and counseling course is made up of no more than fifteen students. Developmental studies counselors conduct these classes. The primary purpose of the course is to enhance the individual student's self-concept or self-image. Through interpersonal relationships with other members of the group he comes to value his opinions and those of others. The course outline includes such topics as getting acquainted with other members of the class, orientation to college and the life of the college student, personal concerns of students, career planning, and individual counseling sessions.

While not part of the developmental studies program at El Centro, the activities and purposes of the Urban Progress with Education Project (UP) determine to a great extent the kinds of student services provided by the developmental studies division. UP is a mobile counseling project funded jointly by the national Talent Search program and the Dallas County Community College District. Beginning the same year the developmental studies division was organized, the UP project has tried to recruit ghetto-environment young people and place them in postsecondary educational institutions. The project's target population lives in economically and socially deprived areas of the city. Eighty-five percent of those placed in college by UP during the first three years were black, 15 percent chicano, and 5 percent white. The outreach program will be extended in 1972–1973 to returning veterans and

29

American Indians living in the metropolitan area. The number of Indians residing in the area has been estimated as ranging from a U.S. Census Bureau figure of 4,638 to a Bureau of Indian Affairs figure of 11,000.

The ability of the UP to reach its target population has been increased through its use of a mobile counseling center. A self-contained van or truck accommodating two staff counselors and six student peer counselors circulates throughout the target area searching out young people who are unaware of the postsecondary educational opportunities available to them. During its three-year history the project has placed more than one thousand students in colleges and contacted an estimated three to four thousand people. The mean ACT composite score of all clients of the UP during the first three years was 8.9. Those who enroll at El Centro become candidates for the developmental studies program.

Preliminary follow-up studies on students who go back to the community college after the freshman year show a return rate of approximately 33 percent. By contrast, more than 50 percent of UP clients have returned for a second year of work. Andrew Goodrich, Minority Research Director of the American Association of Junior Colleges, reports that the nationwide return rate of minority students to community colleges after one year is only one in nine. Thus, the return rate of UP students is extremely favorable when compared to the national rate.

The A through F grading system used at El Centro is based on a four-point system. In addition, a "P" grade denoting "progress" is awarded to the student who in the opinion of the instructor has made significant progress in the course. The instructor and the student agree on the decision to award the P grade. The student is then allowed to enroll in the course again in an attempt to earn credit. If he does not reenroll, however, the grade does not revert to F, and the student's record will continue to carry the P grade.

With the exception of a brief description of the developmental studies program and several supplementary services, few data of a formal evaluation nature have been compiled at El Centro.

SAN ANTONIO COLLEGE

Students identified as high-risk at San Antonio College are required to successfully complete an interdepartmental program of developmental studies. Factors considered in the placement of students in developmental studies are college entrance examination scores and, to a lesser extent, high school grades. The student who scores 11.0 or below on the composite of the American College Test (ACT) or 630 or below on the combined verbal and quantitative portion of the College Entrance Examination Board's Scholastic Aptitude Test (SAT) is considered a candidate for developmental studies. The courses in which the student is placed are determined by a counselor who interviews the student when he enters college. In preparing the semester program the counselor considers the student's interests, aptitudes, and abilities. The student may be placed solely in developmental studies courses or he may take both developmental studies and other courses in a vocational, academic, or technical program.

Generally, from nine to eleven departments are involved in teaching high-risk students each semester. A representative or coordinator for developmental courses is designated in each department. This individual most often is the department chairman or an instructor who is assigned the responsibility by the chairman. The representative coordinates the remedial course efforts within the department and acts as a liason for the overall coordinator of developmental studies. Each department representative also serves as a member of a committee for developmental studies. For example, during the 1970–1971 academic year the committee met with the coordinator of developmental studies on several occasions to draft the "philosophy, principles, plans, recommendations, and goals" for the program. One recommendation made by the committee in the spring of 1971 was that the developmental studies program retain its interdepartmental structure in order that "course content [may] be controlled by the specialized faculty members" within the various departments at the college.

The coordinator of developmental studies also serves as chairman of one department. Most students enrolled in his department are also enrolled in developmental studies. While the coordinator of the program attempts to maintain communication and to exercise a degree of control over the developmental studies courses, each department largely determines the content, methodology, and direction of the remedial courses it teaches.

Approximately one hundred instructors are involved in teaching high-risk students during a semester at San Antonio College. Though certain instructors volunteer for or are assigned remedial courses every semester, the teaching assignment is generally rotated among staff members in each department. A slightly different approach is used in the mathematics department where, when possible, each instructor is assigned at least one developmental studies course.

The subject areas represented in developmental studies include psychology, reading, humanities, English, mathematics, sociology, history, business technology, business administration, natural science, and speech. With the exception of a two-semester course taught by each of the departments of mathematics, humanities, and natural science, a single course is taught by each department. No more than twelve semester hours of credit in developmental courses may count toward the associate degree and these must be for elective credit only.

The primary objective of the developmental studies program at San Antonio is stated as preparing "students to succeed in regular academic or technical courses." Accordingly, the qualification for entering a regular program is stated in the college catalog as follows: "After a student demonstrates satisfactory performance in completing the recommended program of . . . [developmental studies] with at least a 'C' average, he may be admitted by approval of a department chairman or a technical counselor to the curriculum of the student's choice."

No counselors are assigned specifically to the developmental studies program or to high-risk students. A student may confer with the counselor who interviewed him when he arrived, or the student may seek advice from any other counselor on the college staff. Students enrolled in the developmental studies program, however, typically view their respective psychology instructors as their counselors during the initial semester of college attendance.

The original purpose of the psychology course was to provide an orientation to college. That goal has since been expanded to make the course a "human relations lab for social adaptation." Two added purposes are to assist the student in developing a positive self-concept and to introduce possible vocations and the necessary adjustments required in each case. In providing an orientation to college, the psychology instructor tries to help the student become aware of the academic and psychological adjustments required for a successful college experience. This adjustment might involve developing proper study skills, implementing motivational techniques, exploring goal-setting methods, and learning to adjust to new social roles. The topic on developing a positive self-concept entails the study of values, use of psychodramas, sensitivity training, personal counseling, and administration of the Guilford-Zimmerman Temperament Scale. Vocational adjustment includes a study of the philosophical foundations of work values, a review of occupational literature, a research paper on an occupation, and the administration of the Kuder Occupational Interest Survey and the Otis-Lennon Mental Ability Test.

The psychology instructor is also the academic advisor for the students enrolled in his classes and is responsible for conducting an interview with each student at the conclusion of the semester. A course recommendation card is prepared by the instructor for the student. Depending on the grades earned by the student the psychology instructor may recommend that the student enroll in further developmental studies or in a regular college program of studies.

The greatest number of course sections is provided in English, reading, psychology, and mathematics. English is considered to be basically a review course with emphasis on the fundamentals of grammar, pronunciation, spelling, vocabulary, punctuation, and sentence structure. A bilingual approach may be used in English classes for students deficient in this area. The reading course is designed for the student with poor reading skills. Emphasis is placed on comprehension, vocabulary, and study skills. Special reading classes which utilize individualized methods of diagnosis and instruction are provided for students extremely deficient in reading. In order to ensure personal contact between student and teacher some classes consist of no more than ten students. Though the mathematics course is listed in various publications as a remedial course, entering students lacking required algebra credits are also required to enroll in the course. For students who experience difficulties in remedial courses peer tutors are available at no charge in the subject areas of mathematics, English, and natural science.

Enrollment in the developmental studies program at

Table 3

POPULATION CHARACTERISTICS OF SAN ANTONIO DEVELOPMENTAL STUDIES PROGRAM

Year	Program Size[a]	Sample Size Original N	Sample Size Original %	Sample Size Final N	Sample Size Final %	Mean ACT Composite Score of Sample	Race-Ethnic Composition (Percent)[b] Black	White	Chicano	Other
1969–1970	661	70	11	68	10	10.8	..	..	..	..
1970–1971	872	54	6	50	6	11.1	..	..	..	..
1971–1972	1,219	115	9	71	6	10.5	10	25	65	..

[a] Includes only full-time remedial students.
[b] Race-ethnic data not available for 1969–1970 and 1970–1971 groups.

San Antonio increased in each of the years included in the study, as shown in Table 3. Mean ACT composite scores were: 10.2 for chicanos, 11.8 for whites, and 9.6 for blacks. The mean ACT composite score for the entire group was 10.5. The race-ethnic makeup of the total school enrollment in 1971–1972, as shown by school records, was 42 percent chicano, 47 percent white, 7 percent black, and 4 percent other or unknown classification. No special recruitment practices exist for high-risk students beyond that of maintaining communications with the area high schools and with officials in public and quasi-public agencies which might refer prospective students to the college.

The grading system at San Antonio is based on a four-point system, as shown in Table 4.

The I grade may be awarded when the student has a passing course average but was unable to complete the requirements of the course for justifiable reasons. Unless the work is completed within 120 days the grade becomes an F. The IP grade may be used if there is reason to believe that the student has the potential to satisfactorily complete the requirements of the course with additional time. The IP is implemented at the discretion of the individual department.

The standard of work required of the student in order for him to remain in good academic standing is determined from a sliding scale. For example, the student who is enrolled for nine semester hours must pass at least five of those hours and earn a minimum of thirteen grade points. The student who enrolls in sixteen semester hours of course work must pass ten of those hours and earn a minimum of twenty-three grade points. Evaluation of academic performance is based on the current semester, provided the student is enrolled in at least nine semester hours, rather than on a cumulative gradepoint average. However, a cumulative GPA is required for attaining the associate degree.

The Programs

Table 4
Grading System at San Antonio College

Grade	Interpretation	Gradepoint Value
A	Excellent	4 points
B	Good	3 points
C	Average	2 points
D	Pass	1 point
F, WF	Failure, Withdrawn (failing)	0 points
I	Incomplete	Not computed
IP	In progress	Not computed
WP	Withdrawn (passing)	Not computed
NC	Non-credit	Not computed

SOUTHEASTERN COMMUNITY COLLEGE

The Advancement Studies Program, commonly referred to as ASP, is an experimental program for the non-traditional or high-risk student at Southeastern Community College in Whiteville, North Carolina. The program is considered by the college as experimental because by design it is limited to a small number of students. In 1969–1970, the initial year of the program, enrollment in ASP was limited to only twenty-five students. In 1970–1971 and 1971–1972 enrollment was expanded to fifty and seventy-five students, respectively. By controlling the enrollment the ASP staff and college administration contend that effective teaching-learning strategies can be developed and refined.

From its inception the ASP was an experiment in remedial education. Entering students each year who were identified as potentially low academic achievers constituted a pool from which students were randomly selected to go into ASP. A like number from the remaining high-risk students were randomly selected as a control group which was subjected to more traditional approaches to instruction.

In the developmental studies program the student is allowed to a great extent to progress at his own rate. Behavioral objectives are stated for each of the courses included in ASP. Learning is individualized through the use of self-instructional packages, programmed materials, and various audio-tutorial methods. Learning activities are organized so as to be self-contained independent units of study.

The ASP staff lists the following goals of program: (1) to place the student at the center of the learning process by increasing learning activity options and providing opportunities for students to design portions of the curriculum; (2) to recognize and respond to individual differences in skills, values, and learning styles through a flexible curriculum which permits learning at different rates and in different ways; (3) to relate to students with openness and respect and to provide a supportive climate for learning; (4) to provide students positive reinforcement and opportunities for success experiences; (5) to provide a curriculum which will be experiential and process-oriented; (6) to provide an interdisciplinary approach to the teaching-learning process; and (7) to make the community an extension of the classroom.

Initially the program was called Experiment in Advancement Studies. Students selected for EAS were blocked into a twenty-hour week, with English and psychology being the core of the program. Since that first year the program has been expanded to include science, reading, and mathematics. The math course, however, is not taught by the ASP staff. Extensive use has been made of team teaching, role-playing, simulations, small and large group process sessions, sensitivity games, and community projects. Presently, two full-time paraprofessional staff members fill the nonauthoritarian roles of both counselor and tutor. Designated as "tutor-counselors," they attend classes with students enrolled in the program. The tutor-counselors work closely not only with students individually and in small groups but also with the instructors. Because the tutor-counselor is not charged with the responsibility of assigning grades, students relate well with him. During the 1971–1972 academic year there were a black and a white tutor-counselor. One held a degree from a four-year college while the other had completed the ASP program with an associate of arts degree.

Other than the two paraprofessional tutor-counselors there are no regular college counselors assigned exclusively to the developmental studies program. The regular college counselors, however, administer the testing program for placement and advisement purposes to all entering freshmen at the college. Those students who score in the lowest tertile are required to enroll in some developmental studies while the lower half of the middle tertile are advised strongly to enroll in developmental studies. From this pool of high-risk students the ASP enrollees and the control group enrollees are randomly selected. In addition to the two tutor-counselors, the program has one full-time program coordinator and three instructors.

Students enrolled in the ASP are required to be involved in community service projects. As part of a holistic approach to education, students learn to relate psychology, English, science, math, and reading to projects such as tutoring and counseling elementary school students, working with the mentally retarded, assisting the aged, initiating a Head Start program, and running recycling centers where glass, tin, and aluminum are collected, cleared, packaged, and sold. Students learn to identify problems, research them, devise solutions, and eventually write up the results of the project as term papers in their courses.

A student may leave the program at any time during the year and enter regular college courses. Approximately 50 percent of the students exit the program before the year is over. Most courses count toward graduation from the two-year college. Depending on the four-year college selected, some courses may be accepted for credit by the transfer institution.

The ASP at present consists of three major components. The communications component deals with nonverbal communication processes, the printed aspect of communications, verbal or oral processes, written composition, and finally the electronic media. The second component involves social psychology and the psychology of learning. Included are such topics as relating to others, home and family relationships, career possibilities, community involvement, and leisure-time management. The third major component of ASP is ecological biology, which emphasizes the cultivation of environmental consciousness in each student.

The college grading system uses the traditional A, B, C, D, and F method of evaluating students. However, a student enrolled in ASP is not assigned a permanent grade in a developmental studies course until he attains at least a C grade. He may, however, be assigned an I grade, meaning incomplete, until he reaches the C level.

The race-ethnic compositions of the 1971–1972 developmental studies program and the control group of high-risk students are as follows: of forty students in the ASP sample group, 50 percent were black, 40 percent were white, and 10 percent were Indian; of twenty-four controls, 25 percent were black, 38 percent white, 29 percent Indian, and 8 percent other. Black students were estimated to be 30 percent of all students enrolled in the college. Estimated overall members of minority groups made up about 55 to 60 percent of the total enrollment of both the ASP sample and the control group.

BURLINGTON COUNTY COLLEGE

High-risk students who enter Burlington County College at Pemberton, New Jersey, are required to enroll in developmental studies courses if they have sufficiently low ACT scores and high school grades. Neither criterion in itself is cause for placement in remedial courses.

There is no separately organized program or division of developmental studies. Rather, these courses are taught by instructors in two academic divisions of the college, English and mathematics. The primary purpose of developmental courses at Burlington, as described in the catalog, is "to prepare the student to enroll and achieve in college-level courses. The content of the developmental courses, then, is concerned with the sequence of basic skills and abilities."

Instruction for high-risk students is provided in two sequential courses in English, three sequential courses in mathematics, and two sequential courses in reading. A student may enroll in as few or as many developmental courses as he chooses during one semester. If he is deficient in any subject area, then he must successfully achieve the objectives specified in each of the courses in that area before he can enroll in the first college-level credit course. A student enrolled in developmental courses may at the same time be enrolled in regular credit courses in other subject areas.

For the most part developmental courses are taught each semester by the same instructors, who also generally teach regular credit courses. Behavioral objectives have been developed in all courses, and self-instructional packets have been designed for most of them.

Burlington College is totally committed to individualizing instruction. Self-instructional packages, programmed materials, and auto-tutorial methods have been designed for perhaps 80 percent of the total college program. It is hoped that by the fall of 1973 the college will be completely geared for individualized learning. Continuous registration is another planned development. Students would be able to enroll and complete courses at any time during the year.

The commitment to establishing an educational program that is self-instructional is reinforced by a combination media center and instructional objectives writing center. This center has a full-time staff of three people who assist instructors in writing behavioral objectives and in constructing self-learning packages. The most recent and authoritative literature in the field is contained in this center. Included also are copyrighted materials which instructors in the college have developed.

Both a reading laboratory and a writing laboratory have been established to accommodate the "walk-in" student, the referral type student, and the student who reports to the lab as part of the requirements of the course he is taking. Lab personnel may administer diagnostic tests and then prescribe remedial action for the high-risk student. A special testing center has also been created for students who complete course objectives and wish to be evaluated.

There are no counselors assigned exclusively to high-risk students. Other than a brief orientation session prior to enrollment, a preenrollment interview with a college counselor, and a testing session at entrance, the low-achieving student may have little contact with a counselor. If the student has chosen an academic major or a vocational program, he is assigned to a faculty advisor in that field. The undeclared student is randomly assigned to one of the college counselors. Students may also enroll in a group guidance course as a means of determining educational and career objectives.

The mean ACT composite scores of students enrolled full time in developmental studies in 1969–1970, 1970–1971, and 1971–1972 were 10.8, 10.9, and 10.6, respectively. Race-ethnic data for individuals were not available at Burlington County College. The approximate race-ethnic composition of the college is 91 percent white, 7 percent black, and 2 percent of Spanish-speaking origin.

Grades in regular credit courses are awarded according

to how well the student has obtained the course objectives. The following guidelines are outlined by the college: A—mastery of essential elements, acceptable knowledge of a sampling of related concepts, plus either accomplishment of a special project or demonstrated excellence or originality; B—mastery of essential elements and acceptable knowledge of related concepts; C—mastery of essential elements only; D—acceptable knowledge of a sampling of related concepts only; and F—failure to demonstrate acceptable knowledge of course content. An X grade is assigned when the student has been doing satisfactory work but will not complete the stated objectives of the course by the end of term.

Because developmental courses do not count toward graduation at Burlington and are not computed in a student's GPA, gradepoints are not assigned. However, a grading system which parallels that for regular courses is as follows: O—Outstanding; P—Pass; SP—Satisfactory Progress; U—Unsatisfactory; and I—Incomplete. The grade of P signifies that the student is ready to proceed to the next course.

The approach to instruction at Burlington can be illustrated by examining the developmental mathematics program (Burris and Schroeder, 1971), which consists of three sequential courses designed to prepare the student for college-level work in mathematics. The student is placed in developmental math by a counselor who considers the student's ACT math score, his math background, and his academic or career aspirations. The student is given a diagnostic test by the math department in order to determine the level or course in which he should be placed. For example, the first course, Basic Math, is presented in the independent study mode in the math lab. The student listens to a tape that is accompanied by a test-workbook. He performs the prescribed tasks and then takes a posttest on the material. He must achieve at least 80 percent on the posttest in order to move to the next subunit. After completing all the units in the course the student again takes the placement test.

The second course in developmental math is Beginning Algebra. The two modes of available study are independent study and seminar. Three learning-strategy options are available: a programmed text, an audio-tape workbook, and a standard text. The third level of developmental math, Intermediate Algebra, utilizes three modes of instruction. First, large groups are used for presentations of concepts. Second, seminars are used for reinforcement of large group presentations. Third, independent study is supplemented with programmed texts and a tape-workbook presentation. Testing is done in a special math lab consisting of appropriate materials, tutors, learning aids, a study center, and a testing center. Carrels contain a carousel slide projector, film-loop projector, electronic desk calculator, and cassette tape recorder.

3

ASKING THE RIGHT
QUESTIONS

There are many ways to measure a program's effectiveness. Many colleges discuss the "success" of their programs for high-risk students by citing the number of courses available to such students or the number of teachers assigned to them. Some schools simply emphasize the amount of money being expended on the effort to serve high-risk students. And still others point to the comments of instructors as "real measures" of program effectiveness.

In this study, we sought to go beyond these types of assessment. We decided to look at: (1) academic performance of high-risk students as measured by mean gradepoint average (GPA) at selected intervals in the student's collegiate career; (2) persistence as measured by completion of semesters subsequent to initial enrollment period; and (3) students' attitudes toward or degree of satisfaction with counseling, instruction, and the total developmental program.

In studies of academic achievement the traditional criterion of performance has been the student's grades (Lavin, 1965). This is not to say that grades are the best or the only criterion of performance. Indeed, much concern has been voiced about the overemphasis on grades as an indicator of academic success. Certainly, there are questions of goals and values involved. Nevertheless, grades as an important index of academic performance cannot be disputed. In addition, existing research defines academic performance almost exclusively in terms of grades. For these reasons the criterion of performance during each period of enrollment was the mean gradepoint average (GPA) of a student enrolled in a developmental program. The GPA was determined not only for the time the student was enrolled solely in a remedial program but throughout his enrollment in college as well. GPA was assessed each semester and cumulatively for the whole college career.

Persistence data, however, may in the long run be a more valid indicator of success in college than GPA. Prediger (1965, p. 62) writes: "In light of the dropout problem in our colleges and universities; it seems appropriate that more attention be paid to persistence in college as a criterion of success. Ultimately, the student's success in college is judged not in terms of his GPA but, rather, in terms of the educational program which he has completed."

If one measure of program effectiveness or college success can be derived from future monetary returns for students, then the evidence is unequivocal that both college persistence and achievement are related to higher earnings and greater economic opportunity (Levin and others, 1971).

While academic performance and persistence of students have been traditional measures of program effectiveness, there has been little empirical research in ascertaining student attitudes as an indicator of program worth. There is some evidence that permanence of learning is greatly affected by the attitudes the student develops (Roueche, 1968). The success of remedial programs is therefore deemed small if students develop an intense dislike for the college, the program, or any aspect of these. It seems then that those charged with administering remedial programs ought to do whatever is necessary to foster positive attitudes toward learning on the part of students. Yet most recently organized programs of developmental studies have been predicated on the assumption that increased emphasis on counseling and instruction, rather than on attitude improvement, will produce successful learning experience for students. For example, the tacit assumption is made in most serious remediation efforts that individual and group counseling will enhance students' chances for academic success. But Berg (1965), Moore (1970), Iffert (1957), and Haettenschwiller (1971) report that students in two- and four-year colleges are generally dissatisfied with counseling services.

Our study measured degree of satisfaction with remedial education programs among students currently enrolled in developmental studies programs as well as among students who had completed the program and gone into regular college-credit programs. Attitude was determined with data gathered through an attitude-assessment instrument administered to representative students.

KEY TERMS

In our study the following terms are defined according to their intended meaning in this investigation. The term *remedial* is used interchangeably with the following words: directed, guided, basic, compensatory, and developmental. The *high-risk student* is also called the low-achieving, low-ability, marginal, educationally handicapped, or remedial student. The terms *community junior college, community college, junior college,* and *two-year college* are used synonymously.

Persistence is measured by the number of semesters completed by full-time students subsequent to initial semester of enrollment. An exception is made for the 1971–1972 academic year when "enrollment" in the second semester becomes the criterion for determining persistence. *Academic performance* is defined as the mean gradepoint average (GPA) of a group of students for a designated semester or the cumultative mean GPA at selected intervals. *Attitude* means degree of satisfaction of students enrolled in remedial or developmental programs with two aspects of the program: (a) counselors and counseling, and (b) instructors and instruction. In addition, a measure of satisfaction with the overall program was obtained by combining the subscales of counseling and instruction.

The *American College Test (ACT)* includes four examinations in the areas of English, mathematics, social science, and natural science. For each of these tests a raw score is determined from the total number of correct responses. The raw scores are converted into standard scores ranging from a low of 1 to a maximum score of 36. The composite score is derived by averaging standard scores on the four tests.

The currently accepted terms of *black, white,* and *chicano* denote Negro-Americans, Anglo-Americans, and Mexican-Americans, respectively. In this report the terms are spelled in the lower case.

The *full-time high-risk student* was the only one eligible for selection as a subject in the study. This student had to have completed, not merely enrolled in, a minimum of nine credit hours of remedial studies during his initial semester in college. For purposes of this study, a student who received a grade of F in a course was still considered to have received credit.

Asking the Right Questions

Credit in this case is a grade which is final and not tentative, such as an I (Incomplete) or P (Progress) grade.

In order for a high-risk student to continue to be considered full-time he must have completed a minimum of nine hours of course credit for each semester of enrollment in college. A student was not considered full-time for a particular semester if he failed to complete the required number of credits during that semester and had not accumulated the required number of credits, as follows:

1st Semester—Completed minimum of nine hours of remedial studies.

2nd Semester—Completed minimum of eighteen hours of course work, nine of which completed this semester. Included in year's total must be minimum of twelve hours of remedial studies. Completed two semesters of enrollment.

1st Year (Cum)—Completed twelve hours of credit in remedial studies and two semesters of enrollment.

3rd Semester—Completed minimum of twenty-seven hours of credit, nine of which completed this semester. Completed three semesters of enrollment.

1½ Years (Cum)—Completed twenty-seven hours of credit and three semesters of enrollment.

4th Semester—Completed thirty-six hours of credit, nine of which completed this semester. Completed four semesters of enrollment.

2 Years (Cum)—Completed thirty-six hours of credit and four semesters of enrollment.

5th Semester—Completed forty-five hours of credit, nine of which completed this semester. Completed five semesters of enrollment.

2½ Years (Cum)—Completed forty-five hours of credit and five semesters of enrollment.

A student could make up the required number of credits at a later date and thereby satisfy the full-time criterion for a cumulative period. He was not, however, considered full-time during the semester in which he earned less than nine credit hours.

SELECTION OF STUDENTS

Students identified by the five community colleges as potentially low academic achievers in the fall school terms of 1969–1970, 1970–1971, and 1971–1972 constituted the populations from which sample subjects were randomly selected. In each case students who had American College Test composite scores of 16 or greater were eliminated in order to obtain a more homogeneous group in terms of this one variable. At Southeastern Community College the total program population was used as the sample. Here the number of students enrolled in the remedial program was sufficiently small to justify this procedure.

In order to compare peristence and academic performance of high-risk students enrolled in remedial programs with those of comparable students enrolled in nonremedial or regular programs, control groups were formed at three of the colleges during the 1971–1972 academic year. At both Burlington County College and San Antonio College all low-ability students are placed in the developmental studies program; hence no control groups were established.

The 1969–1970 group of developmental program students was selected because most of these students have had sufficient time to graduate or complete a program of college study. Subjects identified as potential low-achievers in the fall term of 1970–1971 served as a more recent group for comparative purposes.

OBTAINING DATA

The effectiveness of developmental programs was assessed in terms of the variables of student persistence, academic performance, and student satisfaction. While individual measures for students were required, program effectiveness was assessed in terms of group mean scores. Gradepoint averages and number of semesters of full-time enrollment for both program and control group students were determined through an examination of official grades on permanent record cards located in the college registrar's office or from computer printouts of those grades.

In order to make comparisons among colleges it was necessary to correlate fall and spring semesters and quarter semesters of attendance. Accordingly, the fall and winter term at Burlington and at Southeastern was combined to correspond to the fall semester at South Campus, El Centro, and San Antonio. Similarly, the spring and summer term at Burlington and at Southeastern was combined to correspond to the spring semester at South Campus, El Centro, and San Antonio.

THE QUESTIONS

As indicated earlier, success can be determined by a variety of criteria. In this study we sought answers to the following kinds of "right" questions. At a time when minority students are boycotting remedial programs and claiming that such programs are racist and designed to produce failure, is there a significant difference in persistence and academic performance between students enrolled in such programs and comparable students who did not enroll in the programs? In other words, can a student achieve similar success (or lack of it) without enrollment in a remedial program? Since each of the colleges included in the study employs a different approach to the problem of the high-risk student, are there significant differences in student performance by college? Has any college been more successful than others? And, if so, what factors contributed to this success? Do some students perform better than others in such programs? Can race-ethnic factors be isolated as elements in producing success or failure? What is the attitude toward counseling of students enrolled in remedial programs? Toward instruction? Toward the total program? Does attitude vary from college to college? Is attitude related to persistence and achievement? And is achievement related to attitude?

METHODOLOGICAL NOTE

Since the research reported here was partially supported by the U.S. Office of Education's Bureau of Research, those researchers interested in a complete description of the research design employed, data treatment, and attitude assessment may wish to see the final research report, now in the public domain, and available from ERIC. It is not our purpose to review the research approach here. For further details, see Roueche and Kirk (1972) and Kirk (1972).

4

THE ANSWERS

At each college where a comparison could be made between students enrolled in remedial programs and those not enrolled, remedial students made significantly higher grades than did comparable students in nonremedial programs. As indicated in Table 5, students in remedial programs earned a mean GPA of 2.66, almost three-fourths of a gradepoint higher than the 1.96 mean GPA earned by high-risk students in nonremedial programs. The two groups of students were compared only on first-semester GPAs because spring-semester grades were not available from South Campus and El Centro at the time data were collected from these two colleges. At Southeastern the difference was highly significant (p. <. 01) High-risk students in the developmental program earned almost a B average (2.91), while students in the regular program earned less than a C average.

The study found that black students in remedial programs earned a mean GPA of 2.94 while comparable black

Table 5

Comparison of First-Semester Mean GPAs for 1971–1972 High-Risk Students at Three Colleges

College Race-Ethnic Group	N	1st Semester Mean GPA		F-ratio	Probability
		Remedial Program	Non-remedial Program		
South Campus (total program)	64	2.54	2.13	5.650	.2927
Black	15	2.28	1.90	1.204	
White	44	2.58	2.07	5.697	.0204[b]
El Centro (total program)	44	2.43	1.87	3.628	
Black	26	2.92	1.99	9.127	.0060[a]
White	15	1.98	1.18	1.140	.3057
Southeastern (total program)	64	2.91	1.83	27.446	
Black	26	3.15	2.04	8.056	.0089[a]
White	16	2.71	1.59	9.085	.0062[a]
Indian	11	2.55	1.94	4.897	.0523
Combined	172	2.66	1.96	31.065	
Black	67	2.94	1.98	25.274	.0000[a]
White	84	2.49	1.84	10.565	.0021[a]

[a] Significant at .01 level.
[b] Significant at .05 level.
Note: A probability level (1) of .05 or less was considered an adequate level of significance for chi square and for the F-ratio when one-way analysis of variance was applied to the problem of determining the significance of the difference between mean scores for the groups.

students in nonremedial programs earned no higher than a mean GPA of 1.98 (almost one full letter grade). Likewise, white students in remedial programs earned a mean GPA of 2.49 compared to a mean GPA of 1.84 earned by high-risk white students in nonremedial programs. In both cases students enrolled in developmental studies programs earned strong first-semester "B" averages while like race-ethnic groups in regular college programs earned well below a "C" average. Significant is the fact that black students earned almost half a letter grade higher (2.94) than did white students, who earned a 2.49 GPA.

When the first-semester GPAs of the five remedial groups for the year 1971–1972 were compared, a significant difference was found, as the following figures reveal—Burlington, 2.16; San Antonio, 2.24; El Centro, 2.43; South Campus, 2.54; and Southeastern, 2.91. The total number of students involved was 139. It should be noted that the mean GPA at each of the five colleges was in the C-average range.

For the 1970–1971 remedial groups there were significant differences at every interval except for the first semester (see Table 6). Of special significance is the GPA earned during the vital third semester when high-risk students at each college were, for the most part, in regular college-credit courses. Only at El Centro and Southeastern were students earning a C average.

When GPAs of remedial groups at the five community colleges were compared over a period of two years, significant differences in GPAs among the colleges were found only for the second semester and for the cumulative of two semesters (see Table 7). Only at El Centro and Southeastern did remedial program students earn C averages for the second and fourth semesters of college work. However, even at these two colleges students failed to earn C averages for the third semester, which is usually the first semester of regular college-

Catching Up: Remedial Education

Table 6

COMPARISON OF MEAN GPAs AMONG COLLEGES AT SEMESTER INTERVALS FOR 1970–1971 GROUPS OF REMEDIAL PROGRAM STUDENTS

Semester Interval	N	*Mean GPAs*				
		South Campus	El Centro	San Antonio	South-eastern	Burl-ington
1st semester	116	2.46	2.53	2.14	2.36	2.20
2nd semester	101	2.68	2.17	1.47	2.53	1.98
Cum 2	104	2.63	2.39	1.90	2.45	2.15
3rd semester	75	1.93	2.05	1.42	2.35	1.72
Cum 3	75	2.50	2.44	1.85	2.50	2.01

Table 7

COMPARISON OF MEAN GPAs AT SEMESTER INTERVALS FOR 1969–1970 GROUPS OF REMEDIAL PROGRAM STUDENTS

Semester Interval	N	*Mean GPAs*				
		South Campus	El Centro	San Antonio	South-eastern	Burl-ington
1st semester	133	2.06	2.35	1.86	2.31	2.07
2nd semester	110	1.83	2.26	1.50	2.21	1.80
Cum 2	115	2.01	2.38	1.83	2.25	1.97
3rd semester	82	1.62	1.98	1.39	1.86	1.76
Cum 3	85	1.93	2.20	1.74	2.10	1.99
4th semester	60	1.92	2.36	1.98	2.28	1.99
Cum 4	61	1.99	2.37	2.00	2.18	2.14

Note: Insufficient data for 5th semester and cumulative of 5 semesters.

credit work. A definite reentry shock occurs during this semester among remedial students in each college.

In general, the study found that mean GPA in remedial programs increased from one year's group to the next. For example, in all the colleges, the mean GPA for the 1970–1971 group was higher than that of the 1969–1970 group. Similarly, students in the 1971–1972 programs earned slightly higher mean GPAs than did the 1970–1971 groups.

Students in remedial programs persist in college longer than comparable students in nonremedial programs. In fact, 82 percent of the students enrolled in developmental programs completed at least two semesters while only 70 percent of high-risk students in nonremedial programs completed two semesters. Of special note is the second-semester persistence rate at South Campus. Ninety-four percent of the remedial program students at South Campus persisted into the second semester, compared to 76 percent persistence on the same campus among nonremedial students. None of the other colleges had above 80 percent second-semester persistence. Yet, in each college, remedial program students persisted considerably better than their nonremedial counterparts.

While students in all colleges expressed general satisfaction with counseling, instruction, and total program, some interesting findings emerged. For example, of students currently enrolled in developmental programs, more than 40 percent were either undecided about or dissatisfied with the help they received from counselors in deciding on a major field of study. Many others expressed indecision or dissatisfaction for the occupational, career-related counseling received during their first semester in college. Altogether, 35 percent of all students were either undecided about or dissatisfied with this particular counseling function. Another 30 percent expressed indecision or stated negative feelings about seeking advice from a counselor on personal problems.

Catching Up: Remedial Education

At least 70 percent of the total number of students currently enrolled in remedial programs in all colleges expressed general or high satisfaction with each of the following aspects: help received from counselors in planning the initial semester of courses; availability of counselors for conferences; group counseling and guidance sessions; becoming aware of one's talents and abilities; information about and orientation to college; and the testing program, including personality, vocational, aptitude, and special-interest measures. Some variation was found, however, between colleges. For example, only 61 percent of the students at one college expressed satisfaction with the testing program while 83 percent of the students at another college felt this way.

Forty-one percent of the students currently enrolled in remedial programs replied that no more than half their classes, and in some cases fewer than this, were interesting and stimulating. Two-thirds considered more than half of their instructors to be superior teachers. Ninety-six percent felt that their instructors knew their subject matter well. At least 70 percent of the students studied expressed satisfaction with these aspects of the program: teaching methods of instructors; opportunity to meet privately with their instructors; developing self-confidence to complete a college program; fairness of grading practices; concern of instructors for students; and usefulness of remedial program in overall college work.

Major findings may be summarized as follows: (1) Students in remedial programs earned significantly higher grades than did high-risk students in nonremedial programs. (2) High-risk students of like race-ethnic groups earned higher grades in remedial programs than did those in nonremedial programs. (3) In each college, grades earned by successive year-groups of students enrolled solely or predominantly in courses in developmental studies improved each year. (4) Academic performance of students in remedial programs dropped significantly after they entered regular college programs. Even with the significant decline in student retention acting as a selective or weeding-out factor, the grades earned by remedial students in regular college courses were, with two exceptions, in the D range. (5) Students in remedial programs persisted in college to a greater extent than did high-risk students in non-remedial programs. (6) At each college, students in remedial programs expressed greater satisfaction with the instructor/instructional component of the remedial program than they did with the counselor/counseling component. (7) Based on findings for the 1969–1970 and 1970–1971 academic years, 50 to 54 percent of high-risk students in remedial programs completed a third semester of college. Thirty-five percent of the 1969–1970 group completed two years of study.

5

COMPONENTS OF SUCCESS

When the senior author first examined remedial efforts he made some remarks which still hold true: "With pressures from society to lengthen the educational experience of all students, the low achieving student has become conspicuous in community junior colleges. No semantical niceties will cover or hide the issue. No matter what the student is called, his problem is the same. To the extent that community junior colleges can identify these students and provide meaningful educational experiences for them, the institution has implemented the concept of the open door. If students are so identified and then allowed to fail, the community junior college has adopted a revolving door" (Roueche, 1968, p. 15).

When this assessment was completed, several questions remained unanswered. The most critical one was simply, "Can a two-year college actually remedy student deficiencies?"

Another pressing question was, "Can a community college remedial course rightfully expect to accomplish in one or two semesters what the public schools have failed to accomplish in twelve years?" (Roueche, 1968, pp. 47–48) Both questions strike at the key assumption behind the open-door admissions policy: that the two-year college provides an effective educational program for all students who enroll. In 1968 there was no tangible evidence that community colleges were doing anything positive for nontraditional, high-risk students. Jencks (1968) boldly charged that two-year colleges had not improved the competitive position of the poor in any way. Many community college authorities agreed that programs for nontraditional students were indeed ineffectual and suggested that the two-year college was "attempting to be too many things to too many people." Some suggested that the community college abandon its idealistic democratic stance and concentrate on "those things" it could do best. Still others advocated getting out of developmental education altogether, citing current program ineffectiveness as certain proof that "democracy's college" was not and could not deliver the educational services it advertised.

In the midst of such controversy and debate, community college personnel in various colleges around the country began to look seriously at existing programs for nontraditional students, to scrutinize the assumptions on which programs were organized (if there were any assumptions behind them), and to consider major program surgery and modifications that might better serve their student clientele. It is good that all colleges did not quit or simply conclude, "It is impossible for a community college to effectively serve the high-risk student!" Some individuals believed the college could provide viable programs for such students and set about developing them. The colleges included in this study may be characterized as "colleges who didn't know it couldn't be done."

Catching Up: Remedial Education

There is one very simple conclusion to the study we have just completed—community colleges *can* effectively serve nontraditional, high-risk students. The present investigation not only documents that such students can be retained for several semesters but further contends that students achieve (learn) and develop positive attitudes toward the college and its developmental program. These effective programs have several common denominators, and it is important to identify them here.

FACULTY

It may be difficult for some readers to believe that only five years ago the inexperienced instructor was the one most often found in the remedial classroom. Teaching high-risk students was an onerous assignment, often reflecting the departmental pecking order. The tenured and experienced instructor got first choice of advanced or specialized courses, while the inexperienced teacher was assigned to teach those classes loaded with students who were obviously "not college material." Not only was he not prepared to understand, let alone teach, the nontraditional student, he was probably convinced that most of his high-risk students would not succeed in his classes. Sure enough, most did not do well. Such initial teacher expectations were typically realized by semester's end.

By contrast, instructors in the colleges studied were nearly all "volunteers." They have chosen their current teaching assignment and take great pride in working with the "new" student. Furthermore, instructors in current programs have high expectations for their students. It has been well documented that teacher expectations are closely tied to eventual student achievement (Bloom, 1971; Rosenthal, 1968), and today's instructor openly and honestly communicates positive expectations to his students. One communica-

62

tions teacher reported, "I tell my students they will never make an F in this course and that I will do anything in my power to assist them in successfully completing course requirements. And while I assure them that I expect them to do well, I also must say that they will not be given credit for the course unless they are willing to help themselves. Once the student finds I am for real, that I can be trusted, they reflect better attitudes and more positive motivation."

Perhaps the most important characteristic of current instructors is their total commitment to helping students be successful. The 1973 instructor is an individual who measures his own teaching success in terms of his students' learning success. No longer do teachers view student attrition and low grades as reflections of poor student attitudes and improper motivation. The instructor in the programs we surveyed cares about students and is not embarrassed to convey those feelings to them. A psychology instructor commented, "Teaching *is* people business. If an instructor doesn't like students, he has no reason to ever be in a comprehensive community college. I honestly like and enjoy my students and, believe it or not, I get most satistfaction in working with those students who have never done well before. That is the real challenge and excitement in community college teaching. Hell, anybody can teach a bright student. That's no big deal! All those highly verbal students need are some directions, a timetable, and good books. It takes a bit more to teach a student who looks you in the eye and says, 'I have never liked school and I see no purpose in your course.' That student is the real challenge and it takes an outstanding teacher to turn him around. But that's where the real payoff is to me as a teacher. My kicks come from working with those kids that traditional teachers gave up on a long time ago."

Current instructors may be characterized as honest and open human beings. They do not view their students as objects. They listen well to the suggestions and comments of their students. Not only do they share their learning objectives with their students, but many of them invite students to suggest additional objectives and learning activities. Today's instructor has found that if he can get his students interested in and committed to his subject, their success is practically guaranteed. Our psychology instructor commented on this point.

I had put together a pretty good course on human potential development and was asking students to react to the suggested outline and make recommendations to improve it. Several students looked at the syllabus for about ten minutes, then commented, "There is nothing in here about drugs. We feel we should have at least one or two units on this critical topic." Well, those students not only wrote the learning objectives for our unit on the psychological and physiological effects of drugs but made outstanding suggestions as to important learning activities for that unit. I could never have developed such an exciting unit without their valuable ideas. These same students later developed their own units on marriage and the family and mental health. Their contributions to my teaching have made me a much more effective instructor and it's only recently that I decided I might be able to learn a few things from them. It's hard to believe I could ever have been such a pompous ass!

It would not be correct to characterize current instructors of nontraditional students as being unconcerned with subject matter. They are concerned with content, but they are more concerned with students. While traditional instructors consider themselves subject-matter specialists, this appellation would not fit the faculty included in our study. These teachers are very concerned with developing good attitudes in their learners. More often than not, they are having to undo all the negative attitudes these students have developed toward education in general and toward their subjects in particular. One instructor talked about the need for faculty attention to student affect: "In the most general sense, all instructors are probably anxious to produce a positive attitude toward their particular subject matter. The instructor whose students achieve As but vow never again to read another book or pursue the subject further probably regards himself as a failure. We enter our respective subject areas because we have a deep interest in and high regard for the content. It has personal meaning for us and we want to share this feeling with our students. If instead we only 'turn students off,' we do more damage than we ever dare to admit." The instructor in current programs honestly wants to work on positive attitude development in students. Allowing the student to contribute to course objectives and learning activities is one way to foster better attitudes, but there are other equally effective strategies. One community college instructor has written a booklet describing the steps in constructing a systematic program for changing student attitudes (Wilkerson, 1972). Charles Johnson, director of the Basic Studies Program at South Campus, sums up his teachers this way. "Our faculty are student-oriented. They are here to assist students and they measure their own effectiveness in how well their students succeed. That our students do succeed creates something of a paradox later on because our Basic Studies students keep coming back to visit with us, to touch base if you please. Contrary to what one might expect, they are not eager to leave the program even after they have completed it. Most likely, their experience in Basic Studies represents the first successful educational experience they have ever had." These comments testify to the benefits of positive attitude development in students.

Another developmental teacher was most explicit about the teacher's role in attitude development. He said, "We need teachers who give a damn about other human beings, teachers who aren't afraid to show students that they are real live caring persons. Our faculty have to earn respect from these students and it comes when students learn you are for real."

The personality of these successful instructors resembles that of the

kind of person who has been described by Abraham Maslow as self-actualizing, by Karen Horney as self-realizing, by Gayle Privette as transcendent functioning, and by Carl Rogers as fully functioning. Other humanistic psychologists have described such healthy personalities as open to experience, democratic, accepting, understanding, caring, supporting, approving, loving, nonjudgmental. They tolerate ambiguity; their decisions come from within rather than without; they have a zest for life, for experiencing, for touching, tasting, feeling, knowing. They risk involvement; they reach out for experiences; they are not afraid to encounter others or themselves. They believe that man is basically good, and given the right conditions, will move in positive directions [O'Banion, 1971].

INSTRUCTION

No single instructional method was common to all the programs surveyed. A wide variety of methodologies and teaching strategies is being employed. One thing is true in all programs, however—teachers are no longer standing in front of classrooms and talking to (or, more appropriately, talking at) students. Lecturing may be an appropriate teaching strategy for some students but not for those enrolled in developmental or basic studies programs. Many high-risk students at entry are simply not verbal learners and they are incapable of acquiring knowledge by routine listening or reading. Such students are often reading at a fourth- or fifth-grade level and do not possess the requisite verbal skills to succeed with traditional instruction. This fact alone may serve well to explain the program failures so common a few years ago. Instruction did not accommodate individual students; rather, it practiced techniques found in other programs where student backgrounds and achievement levels were markedly different. Today's instructional endeavors not only accommodate individual differences but also build on good assumptions of student learning.

Most of the teaching strategies employed in the programs actively involve the student in the learning process. Audio-tutorial instruction is frequently used, building on the notion that students learn better by seeing and doing than they ever can by passive listening. Packaged instruction is another common instructional tool, and even though the packages require some verbal ability, most are developed by faculty to help the student with low verbal ability. Both of these methods permit students as much time as they need to successfully learn the necessary materials. Students can proceed at their own pace and not have to *compete* with others in the program.

Tutoring (both student and faculty) is another common instructional strategy in the surveyed programs. The effort here is to put instruction (and counseling) on a personal level, enhancing communications between teacher and student and student and student. In several colleges, second-year (or second-semester) students are employed as tutors. Often these older students have completed the developmental program and serve as living examples of successful students. These student tutors are peers; they understand the language, frustrations, and fears of the entering student and, perhaps most importantly, are able to communicate openly and honestly with him. A feeling of real trust is revealed by nontraditional students toward their peers who tutor them.

Tutoring has three functions, other than assisting the student when he has problems with a unit: First, supportive teaching takes place immediately after the student has made a mistake and is used frequently in the instructional process. Second, crisis teaching is used when student anxiety over failure to learn or slowness to learn reaches high levels. Third, diagnostic teaching is begun when observation shows that the student is in great difficulty and showing no progress.

All these instructional approaches are designed to assist the student when he needs help. Mary Lyons, a fine Basic Studies instructor at South Campus, comments on the developing instructional program on her campus, "You can't do what teachers have always done to these students. Traditional methods of instruction have been dramatically unsuccessful with our nontraditional students. Unlike the traditional college-bound student, our students don't learn well by listening and reading. We must begin our instructional program with that realization. Furthermore, most of our students have been turned off by those traditional approaches that emphasize the authority role of the teacher."

The use of measurable objectives is another common instructional element in most of the programs surveyed. This practice furnishes purposeful direction for both the instructor and the student. The student knows what he is to learn and, more important, he knows why it is important to learn it. As one teacher put it, "Unless a student is clearly able to see the reward at the goal line, he may not want to play the game. We try to provide honest answers to these three questions posed by students: What am I to do? Under what conditions will I do it? How will I know that I have succeeded? It is our obligation to share course objectives with our students. There is no trick-or-treat teaching and testing here."

The instructional program for nontraditional students needs to break course content (learning activities) into small, manageable tasks. Learning activities are selected because of their potential to bring about the achievement of learning objectives. Any activity that might help the student learn is always considered. These graduated sequences, defined as the arrangement of activities so that they gradually approach the behavior expressed by the objective, allow the student to link small steps together until they form the basis for goal attainment. Many methods of instruction are used, and most important, when the student fails, the burden of responsibility is on the instructor and the administration, not just on the student!

SELF-CONCEPT DEVELOPMENT

As indicated earlier, all the programs provide some focus on the personhood development of each student. El Centro, South Campus, and Southeastern strongly emphasize the innate worth of the individual student and his development of a positive self-image. While little research is available on the self-concept of the community college student, it is generally agreed that nontraditional students are characterized by feelings of powerlessness, worthlessness, alienation, and inappropriate adaptive behaviors—unrealistic levels of aspiration, lack of problem-solving skills and experiences, hostility, aggressiveness, and often delinquency.

The low self-concept of community college students derives from comparison of themselves to students in four-year colleges. They typically exhibit less social maturity and autonomy and feel the only way they can equal or surpass their peers is through occupational pursuits or athletic endeavors (Collins, 1967).

A lack of self-confidence is also reflected in the mental state of the high-risk student, particularly that of the male. The male commuter student (when compared to the four-year-college male resident) has a more negative perception of himself and his world. He feels less positive toward his parents.

His attitudes can either be reinforced (hopefully not) or changed through the educational process of the developmental program (Baker, 1971).

The community college high-risk student, then, is often a hesitant, conservative low-achiever with serious self-doubts, lack of confidence, poor mental health, and motivation too low to detect. He asks to be taught but does not really believe he can learn because he has experienced a lifetime of academic failures. While he aspires to self-actualization, he believes he will fail again.

Several programs are endeavoring to develop three behaviors in their students: the ability to recognize and appreciate their own unique talents and abilities; the ability to establish meaningful and lasting human relationships; and the ability to perceive themselves as worthy and valuable human beings. The real focus in these programs is on developing self-directed individuals who gain confidence in their ability to succeed not only in college but in life. Here again, teacher expectations are crucial.

Small group discussions and individual interactions on a one-to-one basis are particularly effective in allowing students an opportunity to see that they are not the only ones with "nontraditional" or "disadvantaged" backgrounds. These tactics help students relate with others in the program as peers. Group acceptance in these sessions is a positive step toward the development of more positive self-concepts. These gatherings furnish both teacher and students with opportunities to reinforce others in the group and thereby develop more acceptable behavior.

It is important to point out that positive self-concept cannot be given to a student. It must be developed, and it can only be developed as the student finds he can do some things well. Success breeds not only success but strong self-concepts as well. The task in the developmental studies programs is to engineer (design) successful learning experiences for all high-risk students. Ruby Herd of El Centro College puts it succinctly. "We try to find the student's strengths and reinforce them immediately. Simultaneously, we try to provide the student with opportunities for success in other areas." The programs deliberately structure activities to ensure student success. The student's realization that he can learn ("I made an A on my communications test. That's the first A I ever made.") is the real key to an improved, positive self-image. Several colleges indicate plans to assess self-concept on a more formal basis and to chart students as they move to more positive self-images.

PROGRAM IMAGE

In a recent study, Meacham (1972) found significant correlations between the perceived images of community colleges and attendance at these colleges by minority students. As one might expect, colleges with "good images" were well attended by minorities. (To a minority student, good image refers to how welcome the student feels; how he is treated by faculty, counselors and clerical personnel; and whether or not he has desirable curriculum choices available to him.) So too is the program image important to recruiting and retaining nontraditional students. A common charge today is that remedial or developmental programs are racist by intent and design. Some of those charges are probably true, but frequently they are false—based on myth and rumor.

In every college studied, student success was enhanced and magnified by enrollment and persistence in the special basic, guided, or developmental studies programs. It is important that the college make available, indeed publicize, data on student retention and achievement. If the program is effective, registrar reports to high school counselors and

71

teachers can do much to promote good program image. On every campus visited, those students who had participated in college developmental studies programs had high praise for the programs and the faculty associated with them. However, some of the colleges surveyed were struggling to overcome minority charges of "racist program" or "dead-end curriculum," and in recent years the enrollment of minority students in special programs at those schools has declined steadily. The maintenance of a positive image is of crucial importance in reaching those students that these programs are designed to serve. Constant evaluation and public dissemination of student retention, achievement, and attitudes is essential to such positive image development. At times, even current evaluation data will not offset negative rumors or charges. Several of the colleges had met with various minority community leaders during the planning stages of their developmental programs and received inputs from those individuals early in the program's history. Perhaps more important, the planners were able to clarify program intent before the program was established and dispel anxieties and fears that such community leaders may have had from their knowledge of similar programs elsewhere. There are no magic wands to wave that will clarify misconceptions that may develop, but keeping the facts before these constituents is an effective strategy for dealing with rumors. At least this technique is serving several colleges very well.

COUNSELING

Critics of student personnel services probably read Chapter Four and concluded, "I knew that guidance and counseling was for the birds. Those students consistently gave low ratings to guidance and counseling." While student awareness of and satisfaction with student personnel services was "low," there are several possible explanations for this finding.

At several colleges, developmental education is approached as a "team" enterprise, and every team has at least one professional counselor in its starting lineup. The counselor member of the team is not referred to as "a counselor"; he is just another key member of the team. It is likely that students at these institutions were actually unaware of the continuing guidance and counseling they received (from counselors and faculty) and simply could not recall a separate encounter with counselors. On the other hand, students may actually be aware of the counselor but still express dissatisfaction with the services or help they receive. There may be a lingering confusion in the student's mind as to the role of the counselor in the total educational experience. Many counselors reported that they spent most of their professional time in routine information dispensing activities—helping students register, reviewing senior institution transfer requirements, helping students fill out financial aid forms, ad infinitum. It is possible that nontraditional students are wanting (and demanding) *more* from student services personnel.

One student at El Centro expressed his good feelings about his counselor. "The thing I like most about him is that he is concerned about *me* and *my* development and *my* progress. My high school teachers were always telling me this or that, advising me on every thought I should have or move that I make. Mr. ———— listens! Man, he listens better than anybody I've ever known. You know, it's real easy to talk, really open up, when you know the other fellow is really listening. I know this—he wants me to make it and I know I will." This comment was a rather typical one from those students who felt they benefited from guidance and counseling. They felt that the counselor was concerned about their development as real

73

persons. Counseling is likely to be most effective and best regarded by students when the perceived purpose of such activity is personhood development. Counselors are too important to the educational mission of such programs to spend most of their time passing out routine information.

INSTITUTIONAL COMMITMENT

A common factor in all colleges studied was a strong commitment to the developmental program. Not only were campus presidents aware of and able to talk intelligently about the objectives and design of these programs, but they were frequently the creators or originators of such efforts for nontraditional students. W. T. Cottingham, president of Southeastern Community College, comments: "It is absurd to speak about a comprehensive community college with an open-door admissions policy without placing high college priority on the design and development of effective educational programs for all our community's students. We have an obligation to these students and we are going to do more for them than 'keep them off the streets' "

Unlike many community colleges which fund programs for high-risk students primarily from available federal sources, these colleges commit their own institutional resources to their programs. Critics of remedial programs have observed that federal curtailment of Title III programs and the Special Services to the Disadvantaged programs would test the real commitment of the two-year college to the nontraditional student, suggesting that many colleges have such programs only because federal dollars are handy but that their own priorities are elsewhere. In fact, some administrators still cynically talk of the questionable practice of spending good dollars on bad programs. The implication here is that college resources are limited and that, given a heavy demand for those resources, a prudent administrator is the one who seriously considers the possible educational return on his investment. Since these high-risk students have not performed well elsewhere, why should one spend precious resources when the "risks are so high?"

Perhaps the risks are not so high. It should be remembered here that student retention (and, in most cases, achievement as well) in the special programs studied consistently exceeded retention and achievement of students in the regular college curriculum. One might even surmise that it is precisely the college's commitment to and investment in such a program that makes possible good educational returns. If the college president or dean believes such programs are likely to fail and withholds support for that reason, he is likely to prove his initial expectations to be correct. All the presidents of the colleges surveyed supported financially, as well as verbally, the programs described in this report. So did other administrative staff. It is impossible to minimize the importance of presidential and staff support in producing effective programs. Administrative leadership may well be the most important factor in the design of programs for nontraditional students.

SEPARATE PROGRAM

A controversial question today relates to program structure. Should the community college organize any program that segregates students from one another, that focuses attention on student differences? Many minority groups have recently insisted that separate programs further reinforce the inferiority feelings of minority students, prolong the time such students must invest in reaching their educational goals, and are often of questionable value to the student. For these and

75

other reasons the abolition of such programs has been advocated by many minority spokesmen. One black student succinctly expressed his feelings on these issues:

> *I was a good solid B student all through high school. I studied hard! I took my books home with me every night. I always completed my assignments on time. I wanted to go to college and wanted to be well prepared when I arrived here. So what happened? I came out in July, took a six-hour test, and two weeks later was told that my test scores were low and that I was strongly advised to enter the developmental program. I am mad about it all. Who says the test knows best what I can or cannot do? And why should I have to spend the time and money again to get what I should have received in high school? Man, I did my best—all that was required— and now I have to do it all again. Why does the student always take the rap for somebody else's failure? And, man . . . I don't even know whether this hot-shot program will ever get me to the curriculum I want. It's a bad rap!*

What are the alternatives? Some persons maintain that individualized instructional development might indeed minimize the need for separate or special programs. This view holds that when community colleges can literally take a student at whatever level he may be upon entry and allow him to proceed at his own pace until he achieves college credit in his chosen curriculum areas, the need for separate programs will be eliminated. Perhaps so, but the student will still be investing more time and money than other students even if he is not segregated. We believe such refined instructional development in community colleges is still a future possibility, but few institutions are so adept at instruction at present that the need for separate programs is obviated. In instructional development, as in teaching nontraditional students, the teacher is the key, and not all community college teachers are yet ready to accept personal responsibility for the achievement of their students. We agree that if all teachers were the caring, open, honest human beings we described earlier in this chapter, we could quickly consider the elimination of separate programs. As most readers already know, such is not the case.

Another factor to keep in mind when discussing the elimination of separation is that most of the programs reported here focus strongly on individual student self-concept development. It is doubtful that such a focus could be maintained without programmatic emphasis. Put another way, not all teachers are yet ready to accept student personhood development as the proper task for a community college teacher. Most faculty are still subject-matter specialists and still derive their greatest satisfaction from teaching advanced courses to already motivated students. The content orientation is still very strong in college parallel programs (even though most transfer faculty espouse "appreciation" objectives as the important goals for their classes), and this orientation probably will not change dramatically until graduate teacher-preparation programs expand their traditional subject-matter orientation to include more attention to the student. To speak directly, few teachers learn how to teach as a result of graduate preparation. On the contrary, faculty learn a good deal of content, most of which they will never teach in the two-year college.

The single most disconcerting aspect of our findings bears upon the question of whether or not a separate program is needed or justified. The reader will remember that, at every college, students suffered a rather dramatic loss of gradepoint average the semester they left the developmental program (although it should be noted that scores of those who persisted were higher in fourth semester than in second). Stated another way, attrition accelerated and achievement declined as students entered traditional college classes.

Catching Up: Remedial Education

Some will explain this phenomena as nothing more than traditional transfer shock, noting that junior college students have always suffered GPA losses after transfering to senior institutions. The new environment obviously contributes to this transfer shock. But we suggest that there may be other interpretations of the dramatic reduction in the student's gradepoint average as he enrolls in regular college courses.

First of all, he is encountering teachers whose value systems are different from those of faculty he associated with in his developmental program. These "traditional" faculty may have little regard for students who come out of programs where "content has been diluted and teachers coddle the students." It may be that regular college faculty do not yet expect such students to succeed in regular courses.

Second, he is returning to a different mode of instruction from that he had in developmental studies. The objectives in all courses are not yet made explicit to students, and teaching variety is not yet commonplace in traditional classes. As one dean observed, "It may be that we are putting students back into an environment that created (or at least contributed to) their educational deprivation in the first place." Traditional methods of teaching (lecture/textbook/discussion) are simply not best for all, or most, students. Perhaps the successful developmental student returns to a procedure that failed him in the public schools and is likely to fail him again.

It is also possible that the developmental student has not (at program's end) developed enough confidence, or the necessary mechanics skills, to succeed in traditional programs. We do not mean reading and writing skills but ability to figure out what the teacher expects and become proficient at "trick-or-treat" classroom teaching.

There are other interpretations that could be made, but in any event, we feel that the community college cannot yet seriously consider the abolition of special developmental programs. Instead, what is probably needed is an entire community college built around the assumptions that have produced such successful developmental studies programs. If we have found ways to motivate, retain, and educate our most difficult clients, why not consider those strategies for the rest of our students? Caring teachers who know how to excite and stimulate students should be available to all students. Cultivating and hiring them must be our long-range goal. Until then, we see no viable alternative to separate programs.

6

PUTTING IT ALL
TOGETHER

It would be erroneous to conclude from this report that the nation's community colleges are effectively serving the needs of high-risk, nontraditional students. Such is not the case! A recent survey of community college programs and priorities found that there was no strong commitment (as reflected in the priorities of presidents) either to the development of programs for disadvantaged students or to the college's role in solving social, economic, or political problems in its service area (Bushnell and Zagaris, 1972, p. 68). *Strategies for Change* concludes that:

> *Most community and junior college faculty are ill-prepared to handle the underachieving or low-aptitude student. Those selected for the job frequently enjoy low seniority and*

no tenure. Such assignments reflect the fact that teaching a remedial course is [still] a low-prestige assignment. The inexperienced faculty member, often fresh out of graduate school, has had little in the way of orientation or training in coping with the special needs of this group of students. Too few resources and inappropriate instructional materials conspire to defeat even the most conscientious instructor. The absence of alternative ways of linking students and tutors, faculty and students, and students with students fuels the fires of frustration [p. 120].

It is important to clarify here that the initial intent of our study was to identify and report on "successful" programs for nontraditional students. We did not survey the field to prepare a state-of-the-art report. While there have been exciting developments in some colleges over the past five years, most community college programs are quite accurately characterized by the comments quoted above. Even though we have identified some truly outstanding individual program efforts, community colleges as a "movement" or major educational force in our society still have a way to go before the open-door concept of the people's college will become a reality. This philosophy is hollow unless the college is committed to providing services and programs for all students who need and can benefit from instruction. The community college is established to serve all persons in the community, not just those who require no educational accommodation in order to succeed.

What *can be concluded* from this report is that community colleges (and other educational institutions as well) can design and implement successful programs for nontraditional, high-risk students. The task is neither ridiculous nor impossible. The quality of other college endeavors is not diluted by providing for the educational needs of these new students. We might even conclude that other programs are enhanced and enriched as a result of successful developmental studies efforts.

RECOMMENDATIONS

The two-year college can make good on the promise of the open door. A few institutions already do. That is the message of our report. More significant, other colleges can also develop effective programs if they have the right institutional and administrative commitment. While there are no secret formulas for successful program development, the following suggestions are offered to those who wish to effectively serve new students.

One: the community college should emphasize and work to achieve its goal of serving all students in its community. This may be an obvious recommendation to most readers, but unless the college is seriously committed to effectively serving nontraditional students, other suggestions will be of little, if any, practical value. Such a commitment should be articulated by the president to staff, faculty, students, and community. Presidential interest in such efforts automatically generates interest elsewhere in the college. When the chief executive places high priority on a program, effective design and implementation are possible, perhaps even probable. Without his support, not much is likely to be accomplished.

Two: only instructors who volunteer to teach nontraditional students should ever be involved in developmental programs. This recommendation simply recognizes the facts of teacher expectations in any learning situation. Program administrators should be careful to look for discrepancies between faculty intellectual concerns and gut-level reactions to high-risk students. President Larnie Horton of Kittrell Junior

College described this problem well in a speech to University of Texas education students in 1971.

> *There are many white "liberals" who discuss in the comfort of their living rooms the terrible plight of blacks and browns. Intellectually, they want to do something to alleviate the problem. Yet, those same individuals may not feel at all comfortable in dealing with blacks and browns on a personal level. As long as they look at the problem impersonally, they are concerned, but they may be ill-equipped to relate on a one-to-one basis with an individual student. It is important to look for congruence in individuals before allowing them to work with minority students. If an individual's gut-level reactions aren't reflective of his verbalizations, he should not be working with such students.*

Students can also provide good feedback on individual teacher/counselor effectiveness and ability to relate to them.

The importance of this recommendation cannot be overemphasized. Quite recently a community college president told us of a faculty member who had published a book on how to teach disadvantaged students. The president continued, "What irony it is! That S.O.B. flunks more of our students than any other of our staff. We are having to get him completely away from such students. I wish that publisher had talked to me before publishing that book." The teacher is still the key! Don't put anybody into this program who doesn't care about students.

Three: a separately organized division of developmental studies should be created with its own staff and administrative head. Though many nontraditional students have encountered success in prior educational experiences, more commonly they have backgrounds of failure and low achievement. If the community college intends to offer educational services to all students, it must accommodate increasingly large numbers of nontraditional students who have performed poorly in previous educational encounters and for whom limited success in a traditional college can be predicted.

Traditional remedial programs have long histories of failure (Roueche, 1968; Bushnell and Zagaris, 1972). Piecemeal approaches simply do not work. A separate division of developmental studies allows faculty and counselors to work with the whole student. This structure permits the creation of an educational program in which students are given a taste of success, helped to develop feelings of individual personal worth, assisted in choosing realistic and attainable career objectives, made to feel they "belong" at the community college, and helped to increase necessary communications skills. Such an integrated program permits group identity for students and facilitates communications between faculty and faculty and faculty and students (Spencer, 1972). Faculty members and counselors function as a community of learning specialists who can collectively know and relate to each individual student as a person.

The focus of the integrated program is on the individual student. By giving each student special attention, by allowing him to work with an honest, caring instructor, by focusing on student success, and by regular social activities, the student feels he belongs at the college. A young black student at El Centro told us: "El Centro is *my* college—well, I should say it is *our* college. I have black brothers who travel a long way to attend here. Some of them drive past two or three other colleges every day. We are the college and we know we are part of it all. I have to say though that this is the first place I have ever felt this way." Perhaps in the future separate programs can be eliminated, but we see no viable alternatives to such arrangements at present.

Putting It All Together

Four: curriculum offerings in developmental programs should be relevant. We are well aware that *relevance* has become just another meaningless term when used in higher education. Yet it is important to design the curriculum around the interests of students if programs are to overcome the negative feelings and attitudes that most high-risk students bring with them to the community college. It is unfortunate that college curricula are determined more by tradition than by current student or societal needs.

For the student who goes to college as a normal part of growing up, traditional curriculum offerings are part of his college expectations. However, the increasing numbers of new students attending community colleges expect to see some payoff—some relationship between what they are asked, indeed required, to learn and the real world. Curriculum dictated by tradition makes little sense to such students. In a recent session with minority students and English faculty at one community college, students raised the following questions: "Who decided that all students should be required to learn only that literature written on a small group of islands off the coast of Western Europe? Haven't other nations contributed anything worthy of our study?" "Why do we always start each literature course with this fellow Beowulf?" "Has anyone in England written anything since 1900?" "Do you honestly expect us to like this stuff? It has no meaning to our world."

Most teachers would immediately retort, "But of course it has meaning." Yet students do not see the relationships. These students are asking honest content questions and faculty must answer them honestly. Fader and McNeil's excellent little book (1968) provides keen insight into the process of building relevance into the curriculum to the point that students not only master content but actually enjoy and, if you please, "appreciate" it.

Most community college instructors, even those honest,

caring ones, still have a basic subject-matter background. Most teachers still consider themselves subject-matter specialists. How ironic that the best strategies for having students master content are always tied to their perceptions of its relevance and value to them! Content should not remain static or assumed.

Nontraditional students need to see why they are required to learn a particular subject. They seek higher education for very practical reasons—they are looking for particular jobs, which will produce higher incomes and the benefits of a better life. They seek a particular program to reach a personal goal. In each learning experience the student needs to see he is getting closer to his goal (Spencer, 1972). Curriculum relevance is essential with these students.

Five: Regular college curriculum offerings should be comprehensive. Some readers may ask, "What does this recommendation have to do with nontraditional students?" There are several answers to that question. Given the practical orientation of these students, they want to see a choice of career opportunities available to them at the conclusion of their developmental programs. Colleges should avoid eliciting charges that only dead-end curriculum choices are available to nontraditional students. Students want access to college-transfer and sophisticated technical programs in addition to traditional occupational offerings.

A community college with a strong college-transfer program and few occupational programs is not in position to effectively serve nontraditional students. Curriculum offerings should be limited only by an insufficient demand for graduates, lack of students for a program, or shortage of program funds. Since most colleges are reimbursed for students who enroll in courses, only program planning or "start-up" monies are usually required of the institution. Not all career-related programs require extravagant expenditures for facilities and equipment. Another consideration in recommending a comprehensive curriculum is the realization that enrollments in community colleges for the past few years have grown as new programs develop. The development of new curricula increases student enrollment and allows the college to give maximum service to both the community and the individual student.

Six: All developmental courses should carry credit for graduation or program certification. More and more colleges are now following this recommendation. The student's interest in and commitment to a developmental program is greatly enhanced when he knows he is earning credit for it. Credit is the easiest thing to give a student and simply reflects student achievement in a given learning task. Improved student motivation and attitude result from this practice.

Seven: grading policies and practices should be nonpunitive. Negative reinforcement and punitive grades have contributed to the lack of success nontraditional students bring with them to the community college. We are not suggesting a letdown of standards; neither are we advocating that students be given credit for anything they do not achieve. Rather, we ask that students be allowed sufficient time (as much as necessary) to accomplish learning tasks. Students receive credit only after they have achieved minimum requirements. They are given nothing. If they do not attain minimum requirements, they receive nothing. They have invested time and money, so there is no need to award them an F to reinforce or document their "failures." As mentioned earlier, several Ivy League colleges have abolished failing grades. Now community colleges can do likewise since those respected academic institutions have pioneered the practice.

Eight: instruction should accommodate individual differences and permit students to learn and proceed at their own paces. Teaching effectiveness is probably the single most important factor in the entire developmental program. Traditional approaches have proven dramatically unsuccessful with nontraditional students. Instructional design must start with the recognition that students deficient in verbal skills do not learn best by listening and reading. (In fact, few individuals do learn *best* by these methods.)

Students need to know what content they are expected to learn (objectives), why (relevance or value) they should learn that material, and where the program will lead them. We recommend that the entire instructional process be developed logically from a determination of what graduates of a developmental program should be able to do. Teachers in traditional college curriculum areas should be asked to specify the proficiencies or competencies students should have as they leave developmental programs.

Once program objectives have been established, many instructional strategies can assist nontraditional students to learn successfully. We contend that individualized instruction is critical to the effectiveness of developmental programs. We are not advocating a particular methodology or technique. Many colleges, including those in our study, incorporate a variety of teaching approaches. All of them permit students variable amounts of times to learn and most allow students to proceed at their own rates.

Learning packages or, simply, "packages" are common in successful programs. These packages incorporate a variety of media, ranging from programmed materials whereby the student proceeds from one frame to another in sequential fashion to individual assignments with specific directions and coordinated presentations using slides and audiotapes, videotapes, simulation models, and games. Since all students learn in different ways, different teaching-learning strategies should be available for student selection (Roueche, 1972).

What we are recommending is an instruction program based on the individual learning need of each student. Individual packages offer an important motivating tool. Since each student knows the learning objectives (what and why) and since he can work through each package as many times as may be necessary, each student should experience a high degree of personal success. Since motivation is directly related to the student's success, this strategy is effective at keeping students in school and positively motivated.

Individualized instruction offers another major benefit to such students: it can be directed to student interests and permit maximum student involvement in learning. The recent development of minicourses or miniunits allows students to choose topics of particular personal interest as appropriate beginning points in courses. When all students do not have to be at precisely the same place in the textbook so that an entire class can listen to an instructor discuss a particular point, a student may be allowed to branch out on a topic that particularly interests him. By following his interests, the student often can learn the desired material quickly and enjoy it. If all learning could be so enjoyed, we could minimize motivational problems (Spencer, 1972, p. 28).

Student tutoring enhances the instructional effort and is valuable to the "giver" and "receiver" alike. Cuyahoga Community College reports increased learning and motivation for both learner and tutor in its tutoring program. Tutors who have completed developmental programs not only serve as successful graduates of such programs but enjoy a peer relationship with developmental learners that no faculty member is likely to achieve.

It is likely that all efforts at personhood development and positive self-concept development are closely related to instructional effectiveness. Only when the individual student realizes he can succeed in his learning endeavors does his self-concept improve. Successful learning experiences are essential to any real personhood development.

Nine: the counseling function in developmental programs must be of real value to students. Ours is not the only study that has detected student unawareness of or disastisfaction with student personnel services; other recent studies have also cited various problems with traditional student services programs (Bushnell and Zagaris, 1972). Counselors must contribute more than the routine information commonly associated with guidance and counseling programs. Counselors have a crucial role to play in developing positive student self-concepts, and that activity is critical in developmental programs. The notion of centralized counseling must be seriously questioned if this objective is to have high priority. Our feeling is that counselors need to get out of their offices and get to know students as real human beings. Some counselors will quickly point out that they often are assigned mundane activities by administrators. We are sure this is often true and reemphasizes the importance of genuine institutional commitment as a first step in effective program development. Counseling has a significant part to play, but, like instruction, it must be based on real needs—not just traditional activities.

Ten: efforts should be made to alleviate the abrupt transition from developmental studies to traditional college curricula. Our hunch is that negative faculty expectation is a major factor in the dramatic reduction in gradepoint average experienced by students entering college-transfer programs. It is worth mentioning that the loss of GPA is the slightest at South Campus, where constant staff inservice development and focus on improved educational programs are the strongest. A student orientation permeates the Tarrant County District, and most instructors there take pride in the successful learning achievements of their students. Staff development activities should be ongoing to develop "readiness" in other instructors who will be called upon to instruct graduates of developmental programs.

Other strategies to reduce student GPA decreases include smaller course loads for students the first semester after departing developmental studies, special tutorial and peer counseling efforts to provide reinforcement and instructional help when the student needs it most, and open laboratories where students can go at any time for assistance in any subject area.

Eleven: once programs are established, effective recruiting strategies should be developed to identify and enroll nontraditional students. A college should not even consider student recruitment unless it has an effective educational program available. Once the program is a reality, however, the college is ready to develop a sound recruitment program. Traditional recruiting strategies (like traditional teaching and counseling) are likely to be ineffective in reaching the nontraditional student. Inviting students to attend "college days," mailing the college newspaper to high school seniors, and visiting Rotary and Lions groups will reach a certain group of students, but probably not the nontraditional ones. Those techniques reach middle-class parents and students.

Students whose families do not think of college do not listen when a recruiter is "talking to the senior class." Average or below-average high school students do not see themselves as qualified or eligible for such opportunities as work-study programs, grants, or loans. Furthermore, when one considers that the average community college student is in his mid-twenties, it is apparent how restricted traditional efforts at recruitment actually are.

Effectively serving the nontraditional student requires much more than the simple willingness to accept him. However, the college should be willing to admit any person past high school age into any program that is appropriate for him.

Catching Up: Remedial Education

An arbitrary barrier of high school diploma or high school equivalency is unreasonable considering the large numbers of Americans who are still without the rudiments of a high school education. Programs should accommodate any adult who did not complete the public school experience.

Adequate financial aid is important in recruiting most nontraditional students. A good financial aid program should take into consideration the total cost of attending college. Tuition, fees, books, clothing, meals, transportation, supplies, and incidental expenses can and should be considered. Federal guidelines for work-study grants and loan programs allow all student costs to be included in calculating need (Spencer, 1972).

Transportation is another common problem of the nontraditional student. The college can usually help solve this difficulty. It may be economically feasible for the college to operate buses. Car pools can be encouraged and often special public transportation routes and fares can be arranged. Student financial aid can also be increased to cover these costs.

Special efforts are needed to contact prospective students who are not planning to attend the community college. Community organizations in disadvantaged areas, such as churches, welfare organizations, and even political groups, should be used for referrals and direct contact with prospects. Advertising in newspapers and on radio and television should be carefully placed to reach the target audience. Spanish-language broadcasts reach Spanish-speaking dropouts, for example.

It has proven most successful to employ minority recruiters to recruit minority students, and use of student recruiters is also effective. Recruiters should visit public places (shopping centers, pool halls, welfare offices, unemployment centers) to meet the prospective nontraditional student. One contact often leads to another brother, sister, or friend. Door-to-door visits by students are reported to be especially effective (Spencer, 1972).

The ethnic background of the recruiter is most important in dealing with persons from lower socioeconomic backgrounds. A general characteristic of such persons is mistrust of outsiders. The poor white, black, or chicano will prefer to deal with one of his own. This congruence is especially needed in dealing with prospective adult students and parents of students. The recruiter must also understand the special characteristics of the persons involved. For instance, a recruiter dealing with chicano students should understand the importance of the father in the student's decision. Likewise, a recruiter dealing with black students should understand the mother's importance. It is so much simpler if the recruiter is from the ethnic group involved.

Other, less generally applicable experiments have also been successful—for instance, starter classes in disadvantaged areas to get individuals used to going to school, provision of transportation, contact with private school counselors, and student recruiting teams.

Efforts to encourage students to continue their education beyond high school should begin several years before graduation. It is too late to start getting students and their families ready for higher education in the spring before or the summer after high school graduation. This early preparation will be very difficult to accomplish since high schools and junior high schools are not directly accessible to community college personnel. All students and their parents must be given more time than is currently afforded by the practice of recruiting high school seniors a few months before they should enter college. More than a few months are required to get students used to the idea of attending college; they must have time to make changes necessary in their lives before they can decide to attend and then select the proper programs (Spencer, 1972).

A FINAL WORD

Now that enrollments in higher education are leveling off, other colleges will once again be admitting students they refused to consider only a few years ago. Practically every college in the nation was still accepting students in the summer of 1972 for the fall term. Yet some prognosticators predict that community college enrollments will double in the coming decade. Already we are seeing signs that lead us to question, perhaps challenge, such predictions. Lombardi's recent recommendation (1971) of a moratorium on new community colleges points out recent enrollment stabilization and cautions against too optimistic or idealistic predictions. Furthermore, few community colleges reported significant enrollment gains in the fall of 1972. If community college enrollment continues to increase, this growth will be due to the development of effective programs for those students who ordinarily would not attend college. As the "people's college," the community college has a bright and promising future, but a refusal to serve all persons in the community will mark its decline and eventual demise. This report offers encouragement and proof that the two-year college can "put it all together." Democracy's college may yet be a reality!

BIBLIOGRAPHY

BAKER, G. A., III. "Bridging the Gap." Unpublished manuscript. Durham, N.C.: National Laboratory for Higher Education, 1971.

BANKS, W. M. A review of *Against the Odds* by William Moore, Jr. *Personnel and Guidance Journal*, 1971, *49*, 499–503.

Basic Studies 1971–72 Report. Fort Worth: South Campus, Tarrant County Junior College, 1972.

BERG, E. H. "Selected Factors Bearing on the Persistence and Academic Performance of Low Ability Students in Four California Junior Colleges." Unpublished doctoral dissertation. University of California, 1965.

BERG, E. H., AND AXTELL, D. *Programs for Disadvantaged Students in California Community Colleges.* Oakland: Peralta Junior College District, 1968 (ERIC ED 026 032).

BLOCKER, C. E., AND OTHERS. *The Two Year College: A Social Synthesis.* Englewood Cliffs, N.J.: Prentice-Hall, 1965.

BLOOM, B. S. *Stability and Change in Human Characterictics.* New York: Wiley, 1964.

Bibliography

BLOOM, B. S., AND OTHERS. *Handbook on Formative and Summative Evaluation of Student Learning.* New York: McGraw-Hill, 1971.

BOSSONE, R. M. *Remedial English Instruction in California Public Junior Colleges—An Analysis and Evaluation of Current Practices.* Sacramento: California State Department of Education, September 1966 (ERIC ED 012 586).

BURRIS, J. AND SCHROEDER, L. "The Developmental Program in Mathematics at Burlington County College." Pemberton, N.J.: Burlington County College, 1971. (mimeographed)

BUSHNELL, D. S., AND ZAGARIS, I. *Strategies for Change: A Report from Project Focus* Washington, D.C.: American Association of Junior Colleges, 1972.

Carnegie Commission on Higher Education. *The Open-Door Colleges: Policies for Community Colleges.* New York: McGraw-Hill, 1970.

CHALGHIAN, S. "Success for Marginal Students." *Junior College Journal,* 1969, *40,* 28–30.

COHEN, A. M. *Dateline '79: Heretical Concepts for the Community College.* Beverly Hills, Calif.: Glencoe Press, 1969.

COHEN, A. M., AND ASSOCIATES. *A Constant Variable.* San Francisco: Jossey-Bass, 1971.

COLEMAN, J. "The Concept of Equality of Educational Opportunity." *Harvard Educational Review,* 1968, *38,* 22.

COLEMAN, J. AND OTHERS. *Equality of Educational Opportunity.* Washington, D.C.: U.S. Department of Health, Education, and Welfare, Office of Education, 1966.

COLLINS, C. *Junior College Student Personnel Programs: What They Are and What They Should Be.* Washington, D.C.: American Association of Junior Colleges, 1967.

Compensatory Education Project, The Advisory Council. *Reaching For the Ideal.* Austin, Texas: Coordinating Board, Texas College and University System, 1971.

Coordinating Board, Texas College and University System. *C B Report,* 1971, *6.*

Coordinating Board, Texas College and University System. *Insti-*

Bibliography

tutions of Higher Education in Texas, 1971–72. Austin, 1972.

CRONBACH, L. J. "Coefficient Alpha and the Internal Structure of Tests." *Psychometrika,* 1951, *16,* 297–334.

CROSS, K. P. *Beyond the Open Door.* San Francisco: Jossey-Bass, 1971.

CROSSLAND, F. E. *Minority Access to College: A Ford Foundation Report.* New York: Schocken, 1971.

DEVALL, W. B. "Community Colleges: A Dissenting View." *Educational Record,* 1968, *49,* 168–172.

Education Daily, May 24, 1971, *4*(100).

FADER, D. N., AND MC NEAL, E. B. *Hooked on Books: Program and Proof.* New York: Berkley Publishing, 1968.

FERRIN, R. I. *Developmental Programs in Midwestern Community Colleges.* Evanston, Ill.: College Entrance Examination Board, February 1971 (ERIC ED 048 848).

GAGE, N. L. "I. Q. Heritability, Race Differences, and Educational Research," *Phi Delta Kappan,* 1972, *53,* 308–312.

GAITHER, L. *A Study of Remedial Students.* Fresno, Calif.: Fresno City College, March 1968 (ERIC ED 025 253).

GLEAZER, E. J., JR. "The Community College: Issues of the 1970's." *Educational Record,* 1970, *51,* 47–52.

GORDON, E. W. *The Higher Education of the Disadvantaged.* Washington, D.C.: U.S. Office of Education, 1967.

GORDON, E. W., AND JABLONSKY, A. *Compensatory Education in the Equalization of Educational Opportunity.* National Conference on Equal Educational Opportunity in American Cities. Sponsored by the U.S. Commission on Civil Rights, November 1967.

GORDON, E. W., AND THOMAS, C. L. *Survey of Institutions of Higher Education Regarding the Existence of Special Programs for Non-Traditional Students.* Reported in S. A. Kendrick and C. L. Thomas, "Transition from School to College." *Review of Educational Research,* 1970, *40,* 169.

GORDON, E. W., AND WILKERSON, D. A. *Compensatory Education for the Disadvantaged.* New York: College Entrance Examination Board, 1966.

HAETTENSCHWILLER, D. L. "Counseling Black College Students in Special Programs." *Personnel and Guidance Journal,* 1971, *50,* 29–35.

HEINKEL, O. A. *Evaluation of a General Studies Program for the Potentially Low Academic Achiever in California Junior Colleges.* Washington, D.C.: Department of Health, Education, and Welfare, April 1970 (ERIC ED 039 881).

IFFERT, R. E. *Retention and Withdrawal of College Students.* Bulletin No. 1. Washington, D.C.: U.S. Department of Health, Education, and Welfare, 1957.

JENCKS, C. "Social Stratification and Higher Education." *Harvard Educational Review,* 1968, *38,* 277–316.

JENCKS, C. AND RIESMAN, D. *The Academic Revolution.* Garden City, N.Y.: Doubleday, 1968.

JENNINGS, F. G. "The Two-Year Stretch." *Change,* 1970, *2,* 15–25.

JENSEN, A. R. "How Much Can We Boost IQ and Scholastic Achievement?" *Harvard Educational Review,* 1969, *39,* 1–23.

KENDRICK, S. A., AND THOMAS, C. L. "Transition from School to College." *Review of Educational Research,* 1970, *40,* 151–179.

KIRK, R. W. "An Assessment of the Effectiveness of Remedial Programs in Selected Urban Junior Colleges in Texas." Unpublished doctoral dissertation. University of Texas at Austin, 1972.

KNOELL, D. M. "Are Our Colleges Really Accessible to the Poor?" *Junior College Journal,* 1968, *39,* 9–11.

KNOELL, D. M. *People Who Need College: A Report On Students We Have Yet to Serve.* Washington, D.C.: American Association of Junior Colleges, 1970.

LACKEY, R. D., AND ROSS, G. *Project* SPEED: *Final Report of a Summer Program to Prepare Educationally Deficient Students for College.* Douglas, Ga.: South Georgia College, 1968 (ERIC ED 024 389).

Bibliography

LAVIN, D. E. *The Prediction of Academic Performance.* New York: Russell Sage, 1965.

LEVIN, H. M., AND OTHERS. "School Achievement and Post-School Success." *Review of Educational Research,* 1971, *41,* 1–16.

LIKERT, R. "A Technique for the Measurement of Attitudes." *Archives of Psychology,* 1932, *22,* 140.

LOSAK, J. G. *An Evaluation of Selected Aspects of a Junior College Remedial Reading-Writing Program.* Miami: Miami-Dade Junior College, November 1968 (ERIC ED 027 021).

LUDWIG, L., AND GOLD, B. K. *The Developmental Studies and Tutorial Programs: A Progress Report.* Los Angeles: Los Angeles City College, April 1969 (ERIC ED 031 231).

LYNES, R. "How Good Are the Junior Colleges?" *Harper's Magazine,* 1966, *233,* 53–60.

MAGER, R. F. *Preparing Instructional Objectives.* Palo Alto: Fearon, 1962.

MEACHAM, P. "Personal and Situational Variables Affecting Junior College Attendance by Black Eligibles: An Exploratory Study." Unpublished doctoral dissertation. University of Texas at Austin, 1972.

MEDSKER, L. L., AND TILLERY, D. *Breaking the Access Barriers: A Profile of Two-Year Colleges.* New York: McGraw-Hill, 1971.

MONROE, C. R. *Profile of the Community College.* San Francisco: Jossey-Bass, 1972.

MOORE, W., JR. *Against the Odds.* San Francisco: Jossey-Bass, 1970.

MOORE, W., JR. *Blind Man on a Freeway.* San Francisco: Jossey-Bass, 1971.

MOSTELLER, F., AND MOYNIHAN, D. P. (Eds.) *On Equality of Educational Opportunity.* New York: Random House, 1972.

National Advisory Council on Education Professions Development. *People for the People's College: Community College Staff Development Priorities for the 70's.* Washington, D.C. The Council Room 308, 1111 20th Street, 20036, 1972.

Bibliography

NEWMAN, F., AND OTHERS. *Report on Higher Education.* Washington, D.C.: U.S. Department of Health, Education and Welfare, 1971.

O'BANION, T. U. "Humanizing Education in the Community College." *Junior College Journal,* 1971, *41,* 45.

PREDIGER, D. J. "Prediction of Persistence in College," *Journal of Counseling Psychology,* 1965, *12,* 62–67.

ROGERS, D. "The Failure of Inner City Schools." *Educational Technology,* 1970, *10,* 27–32.

ROSENTHAL, R. "Self-Fulfilling Prophecy." *Psychology Today,* 1968, *2.*

ROSENTHAL, R. AND JACOBSON, L. *Pygmalion in the Classroom.* New York: Holt, Rinehart and Winston, 1968.

ROUECHE, J. E. "The Junior College Remedial Program." *Junior College Research Review,* 1967, *2,* 2.

ROUECHE, J. E. *Salvage, Redirection, or Custody?* Washington, D.C.: American Association of Junior Colleges, 1968.

ROUECHE, J. E., AND HURLBURT, A. S. "The Open-Door College: Problems of the Low Achiever." *Journal of Higher Education,* 1968, *12.*

ROUECHE. J. E., AND KIRK, R. W. *An Evaluation of Innovative Programs Designed to Increase Persistence and Academic Performance of High Risk Students in Community Colleges.* Project No. 2F066, Contract no. OEC-6-72-0731-(509). Washington, D.C.: U.S. Department of Health, Education and Welfare, Office of Education, 1972.

ROUECHE, J. E., in collaboration with J. C. PITMAN. *A Modest Proposal: Students Can Learn.* San Francisco: Jossey-Bass, 1972.

Santa Barbara City College. *An Analysis of the Effectiveness of Tutorial Assistance in English 42: Performance and Persistence Among Low-Achieving Students.* Santa Barbara, Calif.: Office of Research and Development, Santa Barbara City College, 1970a (ERIC ED 042 442).

Santa Barbara City College. *The Summer Readiness Program: Neighborhood Youth Corps at Santa Barbara City College.* Santa Barbara, Calif.: Office of Research and Development, Santa Barbara City College, 1970b (ERIC ED 042 441).

SCHAFER, M. I. *Implementing the Open Door: Compensatory Education in Florida's Community Colleges. Phase 1: Questionnaire.* Gainesville: Florida Community Junior College Inter-Institutional Research Council, December 1970 (ERIC ED 046 370).

SCHENZ, R. F. "An Investigation of Junior College Courses and Curricula for Students With Low Ability." Unpublished doctoral dissertation. University of California at Los Angeles, 1963.

SHOCKLEY, W. "Dysgenics, Geneticity, Raceology: A Challenge to the Intellectual Responsibility of Educators." *Phi Delta Kappan,* 1972, *53,* 297–307.

SILBERMAN, C. E. *Crisis in the Classroom.* New York: Random House, 1970.

SNYDER, F., AND BLOCKER, C. E. *Persistence of Developmental Students.* Harrisburg, Penn.: Harrisburg Area Community College, 1970 (ERIC ED 042 438).

Southern Regional Education Board. *New Challenges to the Junior Colleges.* Atlanta, Ga., 1970.

SPENCER, T. *Reaching for the Ideal.* A Report of the Advisory Council of the Texas Compensatory Education Project. Austin: Coordinating Board, Texas College and University System, 1972.

STEVENSON, J. L. *Implementing the Open Door: Compensatory Education in Florida's Community Colleges. Phase II: English Composition.* Gainesville: Florida Community Junior College Inter-Institutional Research Council, September 1970 (ERIC ED 042 456).

THOMAS, C. L. *An Estimate of Commitment Level of Colleges and Universities Assisting Disadvantaged Students.* New York: Teachers College, Columbia University, 1969. (mimeographed) Reported in S. A. Kendrick and C. L. Thomas, "Transition from School to College." *Review of Educational Research,* 1970, *40,* 151–179.

Bibliography

THURSTONE, L. L. "Theory of Attitude Measurement." *Psychological Bulletin,* 1929, *36,* 222–241.

WHITE, W. F. *Tactics for Teaching the Disadvantaged.* New York: McGraw-Hill, 1971.

WILKERSON, G. "Shaping Student Affect." Unpublished instructional unit. The University of Texas at Austin, 1972.

WILLINGHAM, W. W. *Free Access to Higher Education.* New York: College Entrance Examination Board, 1970.

INDEX

Index

E

Educationally handicapped students. *See* Students, high-risk

El Centro College, Guided Studies program at, 22–31; counseling for, 73; enrollment in, 25–26; gradepoint average in, 55–56; grading system in, 30–31; identifying students for, 24–25; instructional methods in, 27–29; objectives of, 22–24; and race-ethnic makeup, 25–26; self-concept development in, 29, 69, 71; student attitudes toward, 84; student services in, 24, 29–30; subject areas for, 27; and Urban Progress with Education Project, 29–30

English courses: at El Centro College, 28–29; reading level in, 8; remedial, 6; at San Antonio College, 34

Enrollment in remedial programs: at El Centro College, 25–26; at San Antonio College, 34–36; at Southeastern Community College, 37; at Tarrant County Junior College, 20–21

F

Faculty: recommendations for, 82–83; and remedial education success, 62–66; as volunteers for remedial education, 8, 15, 23, 32, 62–63, 82–83

Full-time student, defined, 48–49

G

GIBBS, P., 68

GORDON, E. W., 6

Gradepoint average: as performance criterion, 46; recommendations concerning, 90–91; related to program image, 72; in

remedial programs, 53–57, 58–59

Grading system: at Burlington County College, 42–43; at El Centro College, 30–31; recommendations concerning, 87; at San Antonio College, 35, 37; at Southeastern Community College, 40; at Tarrant County Junior College, 22

Guided education. *See* Remedial education

H

Harrisburg Area Community College, 7

HERD, R., 71

High-risk students. *See* Students, high-risk

HORTON, L., 82–83

Humanities course, 16–17

I

Instructional methods: at Burlington County College, 41–42; development in, 8; at El Centro College, 27–29; recommendations for, 87–90; and remedial education success, 66–69; at San Antonio College, 34; at Southeastern Community College, 38; at Tarrant County Junior College, 19

J

JENCKS, C., 2, 61

JENNINGS, F. G., 2–3

JOHNSON, C., 65

K

KENDRICK, S. A., 6

L

Los Angeles City College, 7

Low-ability students. *See* Students, high-risk

Index

105

Index